The Greek Legacy

T.M. Robinson

Professor, Departments of Philosophy
and Classics, University of Toronto

Canadian Broadcasting Corporation

The Greek Legacy is based on a five-part radio broadcast that was originally aired in the fall of 1978 as part of CBC's IDEAS series. Producer: Len Scher; Executive Producer of IDEAS: Geraldine Sherman.

Printed in Canada
Published by CBC Merchandising for the Canadian Broadcasting Corporation. Additional copies may be ordered through local booksellers or directly from:
CBC Merchandising
P.O. Box 500
Station "A"
TORONTO, Ontario
M5W 1E6

Acknowledgments

The author wishes to acknowledge with thanks permission to quote from the following copyright sources:

Excerpts from *Agamemnon* from *Aeschylus: The Oresteian Trilogy*, translated by Philip Vellacott (Penguin Classics, Revised edition, 1959) pp. 57-59, 90-91. Philip Vellacott, 1956.

Excerpts from *The Fragments of Archilochus*, by Guy Davenport, reprinted by permission of the University of California Press.

Excerpts from *Greek Lyrics* (1960), translated by Richmond Lattimore, reprinted by permission of the University of Chicago Press.

Excerpts from *Hesiod* (1959), translated by Richmond Lattimore, reprinted by permission of the University of Michigan Press.

Excerpts from Euripides *Hippolytus* from *The Complete Greek Tragedies*, translated by David Grene, reprinted by permission of the University of Chicago Press.

Excerpts from *The Iliad*, translated by Robert Fitzgerald. Copyright ©1974 by Robert Fitzgerald. Reprinted by permission of Doubleday & Company, Inc.

John Mansley Robinson, *An Introduction to Early Greek Philosophy*. Copyright ©1968 by J.M. Robinson. Used by permission of Houghton Mifflin Company.

Excerpts from *Medea* from *Euripides: Medea and Other Plays*, translated by Philip Vellacott (Penguin Classics, 1963) pp. 24-25. Philip Vellacott, 1963.

Excerpts from *The Odyssey*, translated by Robert Fitzerald. Copyright ©1961 by Robert Fitzgerald. Reprinted by permission of Doubleday & Company, Inc.

Excerpts from *Plato: Phaedo* (1975), translated by David Gallop. Copyright ©Oxford University Press. Reprinted by permission of Oxford University Press.

Excerpts from *Plato's Phaedrus* (1952), translated by R. Hackforth, reprinted by permission of Cambridge University Press.

Excerpts from *Plato's Symposium* (1935), translated by Michael Joyce, reprinted by permission of Michael Joyce.

Excerpts from *The Speeches of Aeschines*, translation by D.D. Adams, reprinted by permission of the Loeb Classical Library, Harvard University Press.

Excerpts from *Thucydides: History of the Peloponnesian War*, translated by Rex Warner (Penguin Classics, Revised edition, 1972), pp. 47-48, 129, 163, 75-77, 146-147, 147-148, 313, 161, 212-213, 242, 402-403, 403-404, 407, 495-496.©Rex Warner, 1954.

Excerpts from Euripides *The Trojan Women* from *The Complete Greek Tragedies*, translated by Richmond Lattimore. Reprinted by permission of the University of Chicago Press.

FOR WINNIE

quod petis hic est,
est Ulubris, animus si te non deficit aequus.

Contents

Foreword

This book originated as five one-hour radio-lectures for the Canadian Broadcasting Corporation's "Ideas" Series in October and November, 1978. They are printed substantially as they were written, with a number of minor changes and a few additions; the latter are in all instances parts of the original script that had to be deleted for lack of air-time to accommodate them. I am happy to be able now to publish the complete manuscript. I should also like to take the occasion to thank a number of people for the part they played in the original radio-production: Len Scher, the programme's producer (a model of patience, skill, and benevolent criticism); Geraldine Sherman, Executive Producer of the "Ideas" Series; a number of scholars, short interviews with whom formed part of the original broadcasts—Professors Gregory Nagy, Julian Jaynes, Malcolm McGregor, Virginia Hunter, Desmond Conacher, Ronald Shepherd, and John Thomas; and all others—actors, technicians and secretarial staff—who played a part in the finished product.

The lectures are in no sense meant as a 'general survey' of the culture of Classical Greece. Next to nothing is said, for example, about Art and Architecture, on the simple grounds that in my estimation the introduction of such topics without benefit of visual aids would have been near-valueless, if not positively detrimental. It limits itself to three areas in which the Greeks produced Ideas that I myself have found particularly fruitful: those of socio-political theory and practice, drama, and philosophy. Even in these areas I have been uncompromisingly selective, pretty well confining my attention—after a lengthy Introduction (Lecture One)—to the fifth century, and in particular the later fifth century. (This accounts for my actual omission from discussion of a number of very famous persons, and for my meagre treatment of a number of others—such as Plato and Aristotle; no judgement on my part as to their merits or importance is to be inferred!).

The secondary literature I have unscrupulously drawn upon is usually fairly easily accessible: Andrewes', Kitto's, and Green's general introductions to Greek history and culture; Jones and

Forrest on the rise and institutions of Athens and Sparta; Murray, Kitto, and Vellacott on Greek tragedy; Guthrie on Greek philosophy. To all these authors (and a few others) I am of course greatly indebted; but this will not, I hope, obscure the fact that the book has as its principal objective, not to put together yet another summary of accepted opinion on certain aspects of the Greek achievement, but rather to *let the Greeks speak for themselves* as far as possible, with the minimum of comment from myself. Hence the abnormally extensive amount of *primary* material that is quoted (in translation) in the text. I have tried in all instances to use readable, up-to-date, and reasonably accurate translations; for details see the list of acknowledgments.

I have made no attempt to impose any single pattern of orthography on the translations; each is reprinted as it originally appeared. Translations other than those cited in the list are my own.

My final thanks are due to Rea Wilmshurst, who typed the manuscript with her customary speed, efficiency, and good humour.

Thomas M. Robinson
Toronto, January 10, 1979.

1. Beginnings

Some Saian or other enjoys my shield now.
A very good shield, too.
I had to leave it behind, under a bush.
But *I* got away. So what do *I* care?
Hang the thing! I'll get another just as good.

There are many points at which an account of Greek civilization could begin, and I have chosen the eighth century for two reasons. First, that is the time when writing was re-introduced into Greece, after its disappearance during the Dorian invasions. Secondly, it was a time when large-scale protest at the old order of things was beginning to make itself felt, and irreverent and sardonic opinions, like those of the poet Archilochus above, were being uttered by many who sought a saner and juster world. We are looking at the beginnings of major change in Greek society, and the fact that much of that change, and how people felt about it and reacted to it, will find expression in written language seems to me critical and important. No longer will we have to rely on the important–but mute–testimony of the physical remains; the breath of life will from now on be breathed into the skeletal structure of the civilization by the living word.

Not, I hasten to add, that Greece before the eighth century was simply some lifeless skeleton. The magnificent palaces of Mycenae on the mainland and of Knossos in Crete bear mute witness to two great civilizations flourishing in the middle of

1

the second millennium B.C., one–the Minoan–apparently peace-loving, and given to the enjoyment of the good life, the other–the Mycenaean–more overtly warlike. Of their social and political institutions we know next to nothing, since they collapsed with astonishing rapidity–indeed in less than 200 years–before the onslaughts of invaders from the north, leaving behind them some magnificent palaces, pottery, jewelry, and wall-paintings–and no literature! This is not, of course, to say that they were non-literate. They *had* written language, and one of the most captivating pieces of sleuth-danship in post-war scholarship was its decipherment as an early form of Greek by Michael Ventris. But palace-inventories hardly make for exciting reading, and that is what the so-called 'Linear B' tablets largely consist of. If the Mycenaeans had a literature, it has not survived, and we are left looking at the physical remains of the civilization with the same sense of awe–and loss–that one feels on contemplating the ruins of the Mayan civilization in the Yucatán or the Guatemalan jungle. *They* survive, but the literature does not: and a crucial item in our understanding of the civiliation is missing.

For all its apparent strengths and the would-be impregnability of its palace-fortresses, the Mycenaean civilization had by 1100 fallen before the onslaughts of invaders from the north, whom Greeks themselves called Dorians. Unlike the Mycenaeans, the Dorians had no settled culture of their own, but were probably nomadic, and over the next 400 years or so were gradually absorbed into the society that they conquered. One notable exception was Athens; she, apparently, was never over-run by the Dorians; nor did she ever allow anyone to forget the fact either. This period, from about 1100 to 750, is occasionally referred to as the 'Dark Age' of Greece. I find the term tendentious, as I find the term 'Dark Ages' for the post-Roman epoch tendentious, but it serves its purpose if understood in the sense of 'Age the details of which are obscure'. One major reason for this is that the Dorian invasions were so disruptive as to destroy the country's precarious hold on written language. Over a 400-year span the combined languages of the indigenous inhabitants and those of the various groups of invaders produced the major dialects of Greece of the Classical Period, but in the process the art of writing had been lost. So once more, as in the case of the Mycenaean civilization, we find ourselves without a major means of investigating the details of life during this period. What we can, in fairly broad terms, be sure of in the light of archaeological evidence is that in the early years large numbers fled before the invader from the mainland to the seaboard of Asia Minor, and it is their descendants whom we find settled there during the Classical Period. As the Dark Age continued, the Dorians themselves followed them to Asia Minor in large numbers, adding to the general misgenation. All-in-all, it seems fair to say that the period 1100 to 750 in the history of Greece was one of chaos and disruption, and there was simply never enough stability for any length of time to produce anything even approaching the earlier civilizations of Knossos and Mycenae. But by about 800 the dust was starting to clear. In spite of wide regional differences, a general unity of language and culture was starting to make itself evident in the Aegean world. The disruption of the Dorian invasions has spent itself, and in the relative calm of the 8th century conditions were ripe for a new— though no one could have guessed *how* new—form of civilization.

The ensuing period (i.e. from about the mid-8th century to the year 600 or so) is often referred to as the 'Archaic Age' of Greece, though some historians have preferred to call it the 'Age of Revolution'. Certainly, there are signs of new life that appear with startling suddenness in the mid-8th century, suggesting frustrated energies built up for half a millennium and now at last finding release. The human figure, for example, reappears on pottery—small, at first, and highly stylized and almost lost amid the prevailing geometric designs, but there, nonetheless. With equal suddenness another significant event takes place: *writing* is reintroduced into Greece, in the shape of a variant of the Phoenician alphabet, and with it comes the first writing down of two great epic poems, the *Iliad* and the *Odyssey*, attributed from the beginning to a bard from the Ionian seaboard called Homer. How long the poems go back in oral tradition we cannot be sure of, and scholars dispute the degree to which they reflect the lost world of the Mycenaean age and the world of the epoch in which they were composed. Whatever the truth in this regard (and it may never be fully ascertained), one thing is certain: with the writing down of the poems we ourselves are introduced at a stroke to a major source of information concerning the Greeks of the day: what was calculated to stir their imagination, make them weep, make them laugh, rouse their anger or their pity, startle them, shame them, and in the end—we can be sure—send them off home in that peculiar state of intoxication that comes from direct contact with great art. The poems are too well known to be rehearsed here; suffice it to say that they deal with the fall of Troy to the Greeks (an event which according to some archaeologists may have taken place about 1250 B.C., near the end of the Mycenaean period) and with the adventures of one of the Greek generals, Odysseus, from the time of that fall till the time of his successful return home to his wife, Penelope, on the island of Ithaca. The first thing that strikes the contemporary reader is that the *Odyssey* in particular is so remarkably *un*alien, in spite of its enormous distance from us in time; in fact, those many people who believe that human nature does not change could hardly do better than turn to the *Odyssey* for evidence to bolster their belief. It has everything: a canny and resourceful hero, a strong and faithful heroine, a recognizable set of villains, a rattling good story-line of suspense, with one hair's-breadth escape after another from the forces of nature and the forces of evil, a modest quota of sex and violence, and that warm feeling of completeness and the working out of divine Justice when virtue is finally rewarded and villainy chastised. We may, as I have suggested, know very little about the details of the lives of those who listened to such a story: poor people in particular could not read or write, and could not afford to build their homes of the durable material that is the mainstay of archae-ology. So little or nothing of what they said or constructed has survived. We can be sure, however, that for the great majority of them life was one of unremitting labour for some local squire or ruler with little to vary the monotony, and that their average life-expectancy was rather less than half our own. Were this all that we knew, it would be interesting and important but tantalizingly vague and impersonal; it is the *poems* such people listened to and (presumably) enjoyed that, in my estimation, add the all-important personal dimension and bring the period alive. All five lectures could profitably be spent illustrating this; instead, I shall reluctantly confine myself to three examples.

Let us begin with the account in *Iliad* 6 of the last parting of the Trojan hero, Hector, from his wife, Andromache. What comes through loud and clear are first, the nostalgia of Homer's audience for a long-lost age of heroic, larger-than-life figures and heroic larger-than-life adventures, and secondly (and perhaps more importantly) the fact that Homer's audi-ence is operating on an emotional wave-length so similar to our own that we catch our breath at the apparent minuteness of change across millennia and the depth of our affinity with those who first listened, spell-bound, to the tale:

At this word Hektor whirled and left his hall,

taking the same path he had come by,
along byways, walled lanes, all through the town
until he reached the Skaian Gates, whereby
before long he would issue on the field.
There his warmhearted lady
came to meet him, running: Andrómakhê. . . .
Behind her came her maid, who held the child
against her breast, a rosy baby still,
Hektoridês, the world's delight, as fresh
as a pure shining star. Skamándrios
his father named him; other men would say
Astýanax, "Lord of the Lower Town,"
as Hektor singlehanded guarded Troy.
How brilliantly the warrior smiled, in silence,
his eyes upon the child! Andrómakhê
rested against him, shook away a tear,
and pressed his hand in both her own, to say:

"Oh, my wild one, your bravery will be
your own undoing! No pity for our child,
poor little one, or me in my sad lot—
soon to be deprived of you! Soon, soon
Akhaians as one man will set upon you
and cut you down! Better for me, without you,
to take cold earth for mantle. No more comfort,
no other warmth, after you meet your doom,
but heartbreak only. . . ."
Great Hektor in his shimmering helmet answered:

"Lady, these many things beset my mind
no less than yours. But I should die of shame
before our Trojan men and noblewomen
if like a coward I avoided battle,
nor am I moved to. Long ago I learned
how to be brave, how to go forward always
and to contend for honor. . . .
. . .In my heart and soul I know
a day will come when ancient Ilion falls,

when Priam and the folk of Priam perish.
Not by the Trojans' anguish on that day
am I so overborne in mind—the pain
of Hékabê herself, or Priam king
or of my brothers, many and valorous,
who will have fallen in dust before our enemies—
as by your own grief, when some armed Akhaian
takes you in tears, your free life stripped away.
Before another woman's loom in Argos
it may be you will pass, or at Messêis
or Hypereiê fountain, carrying water,
against your will—iron constraint upon you.
And seeing you in tears, a man may say:
'There is the wife of Hektor, who fought best
of Trojan horsemen when they fought at Troy..
So he may say—and you will ache again
for one man who could keep you out of bondage.
Let me be hidden dark down in my grave
before I hear your cry or know you captive!.'

As he said this, Hektor held out his arms
to take his baby. But the child squirmed round
on the nurse's bosom and began to wail,
terrified by his father's great war helm—
the flashing bronze, the crest with horsehair plume
tossed like a living thing at every nod.
His father began laughing, and his mother
laughed as well. Then from his handsome head
Hektor lifted off his helm and bent
to place it, bright with sunlight, on the ground.
When he had kissed his child and swung him high
to dandle him, he said this prayer:

> "O Zeus
and all immortals, may this child, my son,
become like me a prince among the Trojans.
Let him be strong and brave and rule in power
at Ilion; then someday men will say

'This fellow is far better than his father!'
seeing him home from war, and in his arms
the bloodstained gear of some tall warrior slain—
making his mother proud..'

After this prayer,
into his dear wife's arms he gave his baby,
whom on her fragrant breast
she held and cherished, laughing through her tears.

There may be better statements in literature of love, and heroism, and sense of duty, and human heartbreak, but I am not aware of them. In us, as in Homer's audience, the result is the same, a result best described in an undying line of Vergil:

sunt lacrimae rerum, et mentem mortalia tangunt.
the real has its tears; things mortal touch the heart.

For a complete change of mood, let us turn to a passage in Book 8 of the *Odyssey*. At the court of King Alcinous, the bard Demodocus is regaling the assembled guests with the lubricious account of a trick played on his wife, Aphrodite, and her lover Ares by the lame god, Hephaestus. All the world loves to hear how the underdog wins the bout by skill and stratagem, and a little sex to spice the story makes for entertaining post-prandial listening. We pick up the story at a point where Hephaestus, having used his skills to construct invisible bonds round and above his bed which will tighten automatically when there is strenuous activity on or in it, has trapped Aphrodite and Ares the next time they make use of it. As they lie there in embarrassment, unable to stir a limb, Hephaestus calls out to the other gods in combined triumph and rage:

"O Father Zeus, O gods in bliss forever,
here is indecorous entertainment for you,
Aphroditê, Zeus's daughter,
caught in the act, cheating me, her cripple,

with Arês—devastating Arês.
Cleanlimbed beauty is her joy, not these
bandylegs I came into the world with:
no one to blame but the two gods who bred me!
Come see this pair entwining here
in my own bed! How hot it makes me burn!
I think they may not care to lie much longer,
pressing on one another, passionate lovers;
they'll have enough of bed together soon.
And yet the chain that bagged them holds them down
till Father sends me back my wedding gifts—
all that I poured out for this damned pigeon,
so lovely, and so wanton."

              All the others
were crowding in, now, to the brazen house—
Poseidon who embraces earth, and Hermês
the runner, and Apollo, lord of Distance.
The goddesses stayed home for shame; but these
munificences ranged there in the doorway;
and irrepressible among them all
arose the laughter of the happy gods.
Gazing hard at Hephaistos' handiwork
the gods in turn remarked among themselves:

"No dash in adultery now."

              "The tortoise tags the hare—
Hephaistos catches Arês—and Arês outran the wind."

"The lame god's craft has pinned him. Now shall he
pay what is due from gods taken in cuckoldry."

But who wants a titillating story so unerringly moral in its conclusion? Certainly not Demodocus, nor, one suspects, his listeners, then and now, and a parting comment from Hermes strikes a merry chord in the heart of all who have on occasion dared for love:

9

They made these improving remarks to one another,
but Apollo leaned aside to say to Hermês:

"Son of Zeus, beneficent Wayfinder,
would you accept a coverlet of chain, if only
you lay by Aphroditê's golden side?"

To this the Wayfinder replied, shining:

"Would I not, though, Apollo of distances!
Wrap me in chains three times the weight of these,
come goddesses and gods to see the fun;
only let me lie beside the pale-golden one!"

Finally, some short extracts from *Iliad* 18 in which Homer
describes the details of a great shield made for Achilles by
Hephaestus. Here, in a few deft brush strokes, he paints for
us a vignette of what life in 8th-century Greece and earlier may
well have been like, at any rate some of the time, and for some
of the people (the 'he' of the account is Hephaestus):

He pictured, then, two cities, noble scenes:
weddings in one, and wedding feasts, and brides
led out through town by torchlight from their chambers
amid chorales amid the young men turning
round and round in dances: flutes and harps
among them, keeping up a tune, and women
coming outdoors to stare as they went by.
A crowd, then, in a market place, and there
two men at odds over satisfaction owed
for a murder done: one claimed that all was paid,
and publicly declared it; his opponent
turned the reparation down, and both
demanded a verdict from an arbiter,
as people clamored in support of each,
and criers restrained the crowd. The town elders
sat in a ring, on chairs of polished stone,
the staves of clarion criers in their hands,
with which they sprang up, each to speak in turn,

and in the middle were two golden measures
to be awarded him whose argument
would be the most straightforward.

                Wartime then;
around the other city were emplaced
two columns of besiegers, bright in arms,
as yet divided on which plan they liked:
whether to sack the town, or treat for half
of all the treasure stored in the citadel.
The townsmen would not bow to either: secretly
they armed to break the siege-line. Women and children
stationed on the walls kept watch, with men
whom age disabled. . . .

When they had come to a likely place for ambush,
a river with a watering place for flocks,
they there disposed themselves, compact in bronze.

Two lookouts at a distance from the troops
took their posts, awaiting sight of sheep
and shambling cattle. Both now came in view,
trailed by two herdsmen playing pipes, no hidden
danger in their minds. The ambush party
took them by surprise in a sudden rush;
swiftly they cut off herds and beautiful flocks
of silvery grey sheep, then killed the herdsmen.
When the besiegers from their parleying ground
heard sounds of cattle in stampede, they mounted
behind mettlesome teams, following the sound,
and came up quickly. Battle lines were drawn,
and on the riverbanks the fight began
as each side rifled javelins at the other.
Here then Strife and Uproar joined the fray,
and ghastly Fate, that kept a man with wounds
alive, and one unwounded, and another
dragged by the heels through battle-din in death.
This figure wore a mantle dyed with blood,

and all the figures clashed and fought
like living men, and pulled their dead away.

He put there, too, a king's field. Harvest hands
were swinging whetted scythes to mow the grain,
and stalks were falling along the swath
while binders girded others up in sheaves
with bands of straw—three binders, and behind them
children came as gleaners, proffering
their eager armfuls. And amid them all

the king stood quietly with staff in hand,
happy at heart, upon a new-mown swath.
To one side, under an oak tree his attendants
worked at a harvest banquet. They had killed
a great ox, and were dressing it; their wives
made supper for the hands, with barley strewn.

         A dancing floor as well
he fashioned, like that one in royal Knossos
Daidalos made for the Princess Ariadnê
Here young men and the most desired young girls
were dancing, linked, touching each other's wrists,
the girls in linen, in soft gowns, the men
in well-knit khitons given a gloss with oil;
the girls wore garlands, and the men had daggers
golden-hilted, hung on silver lanyards.
Trained and adept, they circled there with ease
the way a potter sitting at his wheel
will give it a practice twirl between his palms
to see it run; or else, again, in lines
as though in ranks, they moved on one another:
magical dancing! All around, a crowd
stood spellbound as two tumblers led the beat
with spins and handsprings through the company.

I shall be returning on a number of occasions to the whole
question of the role and status of the arts in Greek society,
including the art of poetry such as the above. For the moment

I should like to continue examining those features of 8th-century Greece that were calculated to bring about major change. Significant among these was a sizable population-growth (itself a direct result of the new social stability). Greece, however, then as now simply did not have the arable land to tolerate such increases, and to cope with the surplus population began a policy of colonizing foreign parts that was to last a couple of centuries. New cities were founded all over the northern Mediterranean in particular, from what is now the South of France to the Dardanelles, and on to the shores of the Black Sea. The process was frequently a venture into the unknown, and a major learning process too, as Greeks came into contact (often violent contact) with societies sometimes radically different from their own. It was an age of Discovery, and of trade with areas newly discovered, in which a whole flood of new ideas, from Asia Minor and Egypt in particular, could not help but influence the formation of ideas and attitudes in Greece itself. Two immediately visible examples of this in art and architecture are the massive, and beautiful, stone temples that begin to appear, showing the combined influence of Egyptian temples and the pillared Mycenaean palaces that stood in ruins in the Peloponnese, and the marble and bronze statues of males, (*kouroi*), still angular and stylized like their Egyptian prototypes, but already from the beginning stark naked, softer in outline, and moving in the direction of that naturalism which will be the source of their later fame. In social terms, what we see is the rise of a propertied class, owing any power it has to its own money-making potential rather than to hereditary title. To put it differently, we are looking at the advent of a third, mercantile class, standing somewhere in between the landed aristocracy (themselves the remote descendants of the 'kings' of the Mycenaean period) and the great mass of society who worked for them and, when need arose, helped fight their battles for them. In the semi-feudal, agricultural society that had obtained to this time, capital had remained static, tied up in the landed holdings of the aristocracy. Now, with foreign trade, *liquid* capital was called for urgently, and the introduction into Greece of *coinage* from Lydia (about 600 B.C.) made it readily available for the imaginative risk-taking entrepreneur. Such financial adventurers were in large part the aristocrats themselves, but many were not, and a major force for change in society was born as hereditary land-holders, frequently near-destitute and clinging doggedly to their titles and the plot of inhospitable terrain that went with them, watched upstarts from outside the charmed circle accumulate rapid fortunes in foreign trade, while the upstarts in turn began casting hungry eyes on the *political* power from which they were barred by something so trivial as the blood that happened to flow through their veins.

Two poets, Hesiod and Archilochus, the latter writing about the period 700 to 650 and the former probably a little earlier, give us some idea of the age, in poems which bear the stamp of extraordinary individuality. Archilochus, born about 716 B.C. on the poverty-stricken island of Paros, the illegitimate son, apparently, of an aristocrat and a slave-woman, did what so many must have done in those days and tried his luck by joining a colonizing expedition to the island of Thasos, in the north-east Aegean. Fragments of some of his poems have survived, providing us with a priceless record of life on Greece's expanding frontiers. The fragments are barbed and angry, ranging from distress at his job—that of displacing a local Thracian population that responded by giving the settlers no peace—to distress at the poor success of his love-life. Here are a few of them. First, two lines that catch the tension of what must have been an everlasting military alert:

By spear is kneaded the bread I eat, by spear my Ismanic
wine is won, which I drink, leaning upon my spear.

Or the following vignette of an attack on the settlement:

> There are other shields to be had,
> But not under the spear-hail
> of an artillery attack,
> In the hot work of slaughtering,
> Among the dry racket of javelins,
> Neither seeing nor hearing.

Talking of shields, Archilochus felt no affinity between the squalor of pioneer-work in Thasos and the bygone glories of his ancestors' conquest of Troy. Spartan mothers might tell their sons, parting for war, to return 'either *with* their shield or *on* it', but Archilochus is first and foremost a survivor, as the short poem with which this talk started attests. Like many another survivor, he has a clear notion of the sort of authority he *is* prepared to respect:

> I do despise a tall general,
> One of those swaggerers,
> A curly-haired, cheek-frilled
> whisker dandy.
> For me a proper officer's
> Short and bow-legged,
> Both feet planted well apart,
> Tough in the guts.

We are listening to the voice of the new man, who has as little respect for military tradition as the emerging mercantile class has for the power that stems from lineage.

When not fighting, Archilochus relives the boredom by drinking and whoring. His sexual success is mixed. At one time he can write (describing wish, or habitude, or both: we can't be sure, since all that survives is a fragment of a poem):

> To engage with an insatiable girl,
> Ramming belly against belly,
> Thigh riding against thigh. . . .

15

At another time he gives us a—till then—unmatched vignette or erotic frustration:

> Miserable with desire,
> I lie lifeless,
> My bones shot through
> With thorny anguish
> Sent by the gods.

Several of the fragments suggest even more forcibly than this that, to crown his woes, he had problems with impotence, and we can take leave of him in that sorry state at his guard-post, nodding on his spear between curses and hasty sips of wine and black thoughts like this:

> Long the time, hard the work
> That often goes to heap the wealth
> That drips away—into a whore's belly!

Elsewhere, and probably a little earlier, we have the gentleman-farmer-poet of Boeotia, Hesiod, with a distinctive voice and a distinctive point of view. His mind is neat and tidy, and exhibits an interesting combination of optimism and pessimism about the confused and confusing world in which he finds himself. Like many another, he feels a certain nostalgia for the Mycenaean Age, and he sees his own as degenerate in contrast. But degenerate or not, it is the real world, and he is satisfied that it can be reduced to a fair degree of order and predictability by hard work. He has no tolerance for the abuse of power by those who happen to wield it, and he puts forward a strong plea for the life of Justice as an antidote to social evil. He offers us, however, no *programme* for social reform: just a plea for justice, in hopes of meriting a favourable reward (here or elsewhere) at the hands of Diké, the Goddess Justice, whose all-powerful even-handedness controls the will of Zeus himself. But for all this some significant things are happening here. In his poem *The Theogony* (or,

Origins of the Gods) he reduces to some semblance of order and reason the many chaotic and frequently contradictory myths circulating in his day concerning the Gods and Giants. This search for order, and the satisfaction that it is there to be found, will become a dominant characteristic of later Greek philosophy. As far as the content of the poem is concerned, the violence of the old myths has been drastically minimized (and frequently bowdlerized), and the gods of Mount Olympus, who in the *Iliad* are simply glorified humans in their loves and hates and tantrums and violence and petty jealousies, are passed over in silence—perhaps embarrassed silence. The new man is rather less happy than Homer was to see in the gods the same aristocratic set-up and values that he sees about him in his own world; less ready to accept that the gods are motivated by desires so crude, inconsiderate and cruel as those frequently attributed to them by Homer, and just as frequently exhibited no doubt by individual members of the aristocracy of his day. "No", says Hesiod, writing in his poem *Works and Days*, "Justice *does* pay, and always; the goddess Diké guarantees it." After that clarion-call, it comes as something of a surprise to find that the rest of the poem is not a carefully-articulated programme for social reform, but rather a detailed account of sound farming-techniques and country-virtues. The former approach, however, will appear soon enough. For the moment it is interesting to note our farmer-poet's clear voice and individuality, like that of Archilochus; his anger and disillusionment with much of the *status quo*; and not least his commitment to the peaceable life. If he saw anything romantic about war, violence and the so-called 'military virtues', he certainly kept singularly silent about it. And that makes his, like that of Archilochus, a very new voice indeed.

As we move into the seventh century, we hear poets no less individual, and no less outspoken than Hesiod and Archilochus, and I shall be returning to them later. For the moment I should like to discuss a number of political tendencies in the seventh century that will turn out to be of some significance in Greece's later history. I refer first and foremost to the rise of the *polis*, sometimes translated 'city-state'. For it is in this century that we see the first signs of the weakening of the powers of rulers-by-inheritance (particularly in those areas of the country with easy access to the sea, and to the consequent influx of new and dangerous ideas), and the rise of a new form of society, with a greater sense of collectivity and a greater sharing of communal responsibility. Several reasons can be offered for this: not least the fact that there were not enough hereditary rulers available to govern the many new colonies of which I have spoken. The result was that several powers traditionally retained by an autocratic ruler began to be dispersed among lesser noble families and even among non-nobles, and the tendency developed momentum and apparent irreversibility when—another dramatic result of the re-introduction of writing—the constitutions of the new colonies started to become *codified* in clear and precise terms, so that members of a given collective could begin talking in a meaningful and public way about their *rights*—and could point to written, publicly accessible evidence to substantiate their case. A parallel development in the military sphere was also of some moment. About the year 700 Greek cities began importing from Asia Minor (and very soon began manufacturing on their own) a new and cheap form of heavy armour for infantry. Those who wore it—the 'hoplites' of later fame—were any members of society who could afford it, and were willing to put in hard hours of voluntary service training to serve as an *ad hoc* citizen *infantry* force to match the *cavalry* force that was traditionally controlled by the local hereditary ruler and his retainers. From the very beginning the aristocracy showed a distaste for serving in the new ground-force, to their ultimate discomfiture: as time passed, the hoplites became more and more decisive in the winning of battles, and the cavalry more and more of an expendable luxury, and members of society other than the ruling class had found themselves yet another reason for believing that civic worth was to be valued by something other than heredity.

As the century progressed, the tendency towards more active citizen-participation in the *polis* continued. More and more administrative posts became the right of ordinary citizens, who competed for them and won election by majority vote. But we should not be misled into thinking that democracy in any recognizable form had arrived. Whatever the tendency towards the devolution of *certain* political powers from the control of the aristocracy, the forces of conservatism pulled even more strongly in the opposite direction, at any rate during this early period. (Even in fifth-century Athens, as we shall see, the old propertied families remained a considerable political force to counteract prevailing populist ideals.) Along with this growing polarization between populist and conservative tendencies one should mention another interesting phenomenon of the seventh century, and that is the rise of the 'strong man' or '*tyrannos*' (from which our word 'tyrant' is derived). I have mentioned already how with the opening up of new frontiers and the expansion of trade a new, aggressive and highly successful mercantile class was rapidly coming into being, and it comes as little surprise to find individual members of *this* group and of the more commercially oriented aristocrats seizing by *coup d'état* complete political control of their individual city-states. Their organizational abilities, at least in the commercial field, were usually clear to all from the successes they could show in this area, and there is plenty of evidence to show that in many cases they came to power with a good deal of popular support. Once at the helm, several of them retained both power and popular support by a policy of trade and commerce. I mention the phenomenon to show how, in the seventh century at least, it was far from obvious that the gradual weakening of the power of the ruling noble families would lead to democracy or anything like it. Rule by a successful strong-man will always apparently appeal to a significant section of any group of people, and the seventh century provided perfect conditions for it to come into being and—for a while at least—flourish. While the seeds of democracy may be present in such a situation, it is far from obvious whether they will ever grow into anything.

What in fact happened can wait for future discussion. For the moment I should like to talk about some of the individuals—all of them poets—who voiced their feelings during this period. Like Hesiod and Archilochus, they are all very much individualists; indeed, if we are talking of the seventh century simply in terms of its literary products—and that, in the practical terms of what has survived, means lyric poetry in its several forms—it could fairly be called the Age of Individualism. The poems cover an enormous range, from reaction (*pro* and *con*) to the changing socio-political scene to love-poetry, invective, satire, drinking-songs, at least one diatribe against women, and moody pessimism about life's transience. Let us listen first to the Spartan poet Tyrtaeus, who, unlike Archilochus, is firmly attached to the old heroic ideals and the military virtues:

> No man ever proves himself a good man in war
> unless he can endure to face the blood and the slaughter,
>   go close against the enemy and fight with his hands.
> Here is courage, mankind's finest possession, here is
>   the noblest prize that a young man can endeavor to win,
> and it is a good thing his city and all the people share with him
>   when a man plants his feet and stands in the foremost spears
> relentlessly, all thought of foul flight completely forgotten,
>   and has well trained his heart to be steadfast and to endure,

and with words encourages the man who is stationed beside him.
　　Here is a man who proves himself to be valiant in war.
With a sudden rush he turns to flight the rugged battalions
　　of the enemy, and sustains the beating waves of assault.
And he who so falls among the champions and loses his sweet
　　　　life,
　　so blessing with honor his city, his father, and all his people,
with wounds in his chest, where the spear that he was facing has
　　　　transfixed
　　　　that massive guard of his shield, and gone through his breast-
　　　　plate as well,
why, such a man is lamented alike by the young and the elders,
　　and all his city goes into mourning and grieves for his loss.

　　His tomb is pointed to with pride, and so are his children,
　　and his children's children, and afterward all the race that is
　　　　his.

And now the aristocrat Alcaeus of Mitylene, bitterly critical of any attempts at social reform in his city, and of its *tyrannos* Pittacus, and writing poems ranging from political invective to nature-poetry at its finest. Here, for example, are his views on the local strong-man:

　　This upstart Pittacus, this base-born fool,
　　　　They greet with joy, and great acclaim;
　　And set the willing strong-man up in power,
　　　　To rule their strife-torn and ill-fated state.

And here is his prayer for divine protection from the sea as he sails from the Peloponnese:

　　Be with me now, leaving the Isle of Pelops,
　　mighty sons of Zeus and of Leda, now in
　　kindliness of heart appear to me, Kastor
　　　　and Polydeúkes:

　　you who wander over the wide earth, over
　　all the sea's domain on your flying horses,

easily delivering mortal men from
        death and its terror:

swept in far descent to the strong-built vessel's
masthead, you ride shining upon the cables,
through the weariness of the dark night bringing
        light to the black ship.

And here finally is his description of late summer, which any
visitor to Greece will appreciate:

Wet your whistle with wine now, for the dog star, wheeling
    up the sky,
brings back summer, the time all things are parched under
    the searing heat.
Now the cicada's cry, sweet in the leaves, shrills from be-
    neath his wings.
Now the artichoke flowers, women are lush, ask too much
    of their men,
who grow lank, for the star burning above withers their
    brains and knees.

Like Alcaeus, the poet Mimnermus of Colophon lived in
a city that had been taken over by a strong-man, Gyges of
Lydia. How he reacted to the fact we do not know, but many
have inferred a causal connection between what happened and
the nostalgia and tired pessimism of the few poems of his that
have survived. First a short poem about a warrier of days gone
by:

None could match the strength of him and the pride of his
    courage.
    Thus the tale told of my fathers who saw him there
breaking the massed battalions of armored Lydian horsemen,
    swinging the ashwood spear on the range of the Hermos
    plain.
Pallas Athene, goddess of war, would have found no fault with
    this stark heart in its strength, when at the first-line rush
swift in the blood and staggered collision of armies in battle

all through the raining shafts he fought out a bitter path.
No man ever in the strong encounters of battle was braver
    than he, when he went still in the gleaming light of the sun.

And now, in complete contrast, a few lines on old age and the fading of beauty and desire:

What, then, is life if love the golden is gone? What is pleasure?
    Better to die when the thought of these is lost from my
        heart:
the flattery of surrender, the secret embrace in the darkness.
    These alone are such charming flowers of youth as befall
women and men. But once old age with its sorrows advances
    upon us, it makes a man feeble and ugly alike,
heart worn thin with the hovering expectation of evil,
    lost all joy that comes out of the sight of the sun.
Hateful to boys a man goes then, unfavored of women.
    Such is the thing of sorrow God has made of old age.

On the island of Amorgos, the poet Semonides was writing satire, and dwelling at length on two themes that would prove attractive to satirists for centuries: the 'Vanity of Human Wishes' and (predictably, in a man's universe) 'Women'. The question of the role and status of women in Greek society is something I shall touch on later; for the moment let us just listen to a few extracts from what a seventh-century satirist has to say, and reserve judgment on the broader question.

In the beginning God made various kinds of women
with various minds. He made one from the hairy sow,
that one whose house is smeared with mud, and all within
lies in dishevelment and rolls along the ground,
while the pig-woman in unlaundered clothing sits
unwashed herself among the dunghills, and grows fat.

One [he made] from a weasel—miserable, stinking thing.
There's nothing pretty about her. She has no kind
of charm, no kind of sweetness, and no sex appeal.
She's always crazy to make love and go to bed,

but makes her husband—if she has one—sick, when he
comes near her. And she steals from neighbors. She's
    all bad.
She robs the altar and eats up the sacrifice.

One was begotten from the maned, fastidious mare.
She manages to avoid all housework and the chores
of slaves. She wouldn't touch the mill, or lift a sieve,
or sweep the dung from the house and throw it out of doors,
or kneel by the fire. Afraid the soot will make her dirty.

One was a monkey; and this is the very worst,
most exquisite disaster Zeus has wished on men.
Hers is the ugliest face of all. When such a woman
walks through the village, everybody turns to laugh.
Her neck's so short that she can scarcely turn her head.
Slab-sided, skinny-legged. Oh, unhappy man
who has to take such a disaster in his arms!

One [he made] from a bee. The man is lucky who gets her.
She is the only one no blame can settle on.
A man's life grows and blossoms underneath her touch.
She loves her husband, he loves her, and they grow old
together, while their glorious children rise to fame.
Among the throngs of other women this one shines
as an example. Heavenly grace surrounds her. She
alone takes no delight in sitting with the rest
when the conversation's about sex. It's wives like this
who are God's gift of happiness to mortal men.
These are the thoughtful wives, in every way the best.

But all those other breeds come to us too from God
and by his will. And they stay with us. They won't go.
For women are the biggest single bad thing Zeus
has made for us.

According to one's prejudices, one will no doubt dub the
above articulate misogyny or sophisticated satire or some
combination of the two, but its sentiments were not unique

in the seventh century. Even the gentle Hesiod can calmly say:

> Do not let any sweet-talking woman beguile your good sense
> With the fascinations of her shape. It's your barn she's after.
> Anyone who will trust a woman is trusting flatterers.

As I said earlier, the seventh century was an age of major social and political change, and any change of this order and of such magnitude invariably produces a number of embittered and frustrated people. Some of that frustration, I suspect, was vented in verse like this on an easy target that, due to its enforced non-literacy, could not reply in kind: and that target was, of course, women.

Having said that, I must now qualify myself immediately. While it is true that the door-mat theory of women was generally prevalent in Greek antiquity, there were some startling exceptions to the rule. In the seventh century the island of Lesbos in particular seems to have developed a cultured, sophisticated, and unashamedly hedonistic life-style not unlike the Minoan life-style almost a thousand years before it, and its most famous literary exponent is, as so often, a poet—but a poet with a difference. This time the poet is a woman, Sappho—and apparently a 'citizen of Lesbos' in the contemporary sense as well. The whole question of Greek sexual mores is something that deserves a lecture in itself; for the moment I shall simply note in passing that bisexuality is taken for granted in many of the lyric poets we have been discussing. Not the least of Archilochus's sexual problems, for example, was his relationship with his *boy*-friend Glaucus, and we have already heard Mimnermus lamenting that old age makes him unattractive to boys as well as girls. Lesbianism, by contrast, while apparently part of the life-style on the island of its name, was looked upon elsewhere as an eccentricity, to judge by the following poem of Anacreon of Teos, writing a generation or so after Sappho:

The love god with his golden curls
puts a bright ball into my hand,
shows a girl in her fancy shoes,
    and suggests that I take her.

Not *that* girl—she's the other kind,
one from Lesbos. Disdainfully,
nose turned up at my silver hair,
she makes eyes at the *women*.

Whether Sappho's attraction to women followed upon a
heterosexual phase (we know she was married once, and had
a daughter) or was part of a general bisexuality we do not
know, but her poems of passion are still unmatched for their
beauty, honesty, guiltlessness, and incandescent pain. From
several, I choose two fragmentary poems, and one almost
complete. First a fragment on the Love-god:

Loosener-of-limbs, Love makes me tremble.
He creeps upon me, bitter-sweet but irresistible. . . .

Next, a brief vignette of loneliness:

The moon is down, the constellation
Of the Pleiades has gone to rest;
It's now the middle of the night,
And as the hours pass by,
I lie here, all alone.

Finally, and as a conclusion to these voices from Archaic
Greece, a poem of sexual jealousy, unequalled in its passion,
as she sees her lover sitting next to a man, rather than next
to her.

Like the very gods in my sight is he who
sits where he can look in your eyes, who listens
close to you, to hear the soft voice, its sweetness
    murmur in love and

laughter, all for him. But it breaks my spirit;

underneath my breast all the heart is shaken.
Let me only glance where you are, the voice dies,
       I can say nothing,

but my lips are stricken to silence, underneath my skin the tenuous flame suffuses;
nothing shows in front of my eyes, my ears are
       muted in thunder.

And the sweat breaks running upon me, fever
shakes my body, paler I turn than grass is;
I can feel that I have been changed, I feel that
       death has come near me.

2 Two Societies

In my last talk I discussed the Greece of the eighth and seventh centuries B.C., and attempted to show how it was a period of major social and political change. I now wish to pursue this topic, paying especial attention to two states, Sparta and Athens.

Let us look first at Athens. By the beginning of the sixth century an ugly polarization between the haves and have-nots was making itself felt. This is not to say that the poor at this time were significantly *less* well off than before; just that, with the general expansion of trade in the seventh century and the accumulated—and highly visible—private fortunes that it brought with it, the poor were probably much more sharply aware than before of the degree to which they were dispossessed. One might compare the situation with a modern one, in which a major force for social and political change is the angered sensibilities of millions in the Third World who see daily on television sets the massive affluence of the industrialized West, combined with her apparent determination to maintain the *status quo* more or less as it is and, thanks to her affluence, with apparent power to *do* so—at any rate till just recently. A sixth-century Athenian needed no electronic medium to tell him that the land around him was, with few exeptions, possessed by a very small number of landowners; that many of them had grown significantly wealthier in recent times, and were enjoying the use of unheard-of imported luxuries, thanks to the stimulus of trade and the increase of liquid capital; and that with the increase in wealth had come a greed so apparently insatiable that many of the landholders were prepared to add to their wealth by selling off into slavery any tenant who failed to meet his obligation to pay to his master one-sixth of his produce.

The situation was an ugly one, and by the year 570 or so it had reached a high point of tension, with some of the old, established landowners calling for repression of upstart tenants who were daring to suggest a more equitable distribution of land. The explosion, however, did not come; instead, a mediator acceptable to both groups was appointed, the famous Solon. He was himself a noble, with a background in trade, and something of a reputation for fairness. His first, bold stroke was the cancellation of all debts that tenant-farmers had incurred at the hands of their masters, and all who had been enslaved for debt were brought back home. (This was at any rate the case in theory; how such a gigantic exercise worked out in practice we do not know. But one thing is certain: whether Solon actually introduced formal legislation in the matter or not, we never hear again of any clear instance of a free Athenian's being enslaved for debt.) Among his other reforms three stand out as important in Athens' progress: he established what one might call a People's Court, in which *all* citizens had the right to instigate prosecutions; he gave all citizens the right to sit on juries; and he attempted to re-fashion Athens' class-structure by reference to *wealth* (which still largely meant land) rather than *birth*. Society would now consist of four groups, membership depending on the estimated yield of one's land, rather than on one's pedigree.

On the face of it, all this sounds to modern ears like remarkable progress over what had gone before, but in fact rather less was achieved than at first sight appears. For example, eligibility for public office was restricted to the top two of the four new property-classes, so that the great majority of the citizen-population—not to mention all the slaves, who had no citizen-rights—was still effectively barred from any serious say in the running of their city's affairs. On the other hand, the fact that the top two property-classes (rather than just the old noble families) could run for office meant that fresh blood could now start circulating in the political system—in particular the blood of the new, aggressive, and frequently very perceptive *nouveaux riches* who had made their money in commerce and were anxious to bring their expertise to the political arena, where they might hope to win in time *political* power commensurate with their economic power. Solon the mediator had come up with what was in effect a compromise solution to Athens' problems: the great majority had been given new and important *legal* rights; the new monied and propertied class had won crucial *political* rights; and the old aristocracy, while compelled now to share political power with such upstarts, had the satisfaction of seeing its tightly-knit, exclusive, inward-looking class system, with all its taboos, and privileges, and inner allegiances, just about untouched. But it was a compromise solution which, whether Solon perceived it or not—and I for one doubt whether he guessed the final outcome—bore within it the seeds of significant change.

Such change, however, was still some distance into the future. The immediate results of Solon's legislation were a decade of social chaos, with different aristocratic clans vying for control, and the rise of a dictator, Peisistratus, one of Solon's own relatives, who effectively put an end to it. As was true of many another *tyrannos* ('strong-man') at the time, Peisistratus commanded a good deal of popular support among people who saw little but disadvantage in clan blood-feuds, and in future years some people in democratic Athens would look back upon his one-man reign as some sort of

Heaven on Earth. As we pursue the question of the nature of Athenian democracy, we shall, I think, find this a little less odd than it sounds. For the moment, it is enough to note in passing that during the period of Peisistratus' rule social and constitutional reform may have stood still, but other things did not; in particular it can be said that the public works and the artistic and religious festivals that he initiated and patronized lie at the root of that civic consciousness and pride that will be so much a feature of future Athenian democracy. He was, if you like, an Athens-booster, and was remembered for his commitment to that cause. The point is, I think, an important one. It is easy to think of later Athenian democracy in terms of socio-political achievement, but one cannot without injustice pass over such things as her civic pride, her physical beauty and amenities, her renowned festivals, to which visitors flocked from all over the Greek world, her statuary, her architecture, her dramatic and poetic achievement. And it is here that, by one of the many ironies in Athens' history, much of the credit must be given, not to some far-seeing democratic reformer but to a dictator—Peisistratus.

A third and, many would argue, the most significant figure in Athens' progress towards democracy, was Cleisthenes. The death of the strong-man Peisistratus had been followed by a period of political chaos, in which in (by now) familiar fashion different aristocratic clans had vied bloodily for supremacy. The victor who eventually emerged was Cleisthenes, leader of the Alcmeonid clan, and it soon became clear that major reform was one of his prime objectives. The technique he employed to bring this about had a brilliant and pleasing simplicity to it, though it may seem at first a little complicated. He divided Attica (i.e. Athens and surrounding area) into 170 'boroughs' (or *demes*), and classified each one as respectively coastal, rural, or urban. At the same time he reorganized the entire population into ten 'tribes', making sure that each and every tribe was composed of boroughs from *all three* regions. It was an ingenious move. At a stroke he had ensured that all ten groups into which the population was divided consisted of a very fair *cross-section* of that population. No longer could individual monied and powerful families exercise political clout by calling upon the loyalty of their local retainers, for the newly constituted tribes were now so constituted as to be in three different locations at once, never simply one, and were composed of a general cross-section of the population so similar to the general cross-section found in each of the other nine that the chances of old-style family-domination of any one tribe, let alone several, were cut almost to zero.

But Cleisthenes was not through yet. Not content to rely on his civic reforms to canalize popular loyalty away from the powerful local clans and towards the city-state proper (via the ten tribes), he put teeth into the reforms by organizing the ten tribes as *military* units as well. Physically separated, and all ten of them each in three different locations, the new military units were just about beyond the reach of subversion by particular political groups, however powerful. With no specific loyalty to a faction or particular place, they would, as Cleisthenes saw, tend naturally to direct their loyalty to that *entire* political entity – the city state of Athens – of which they were a part.

Mention should also be made of the practice of *ostracism*, which was introduced into Athenian political life either during Cleisthenes' tenure of office or shortly after. This empowered the Assembly to vote once a year, should they so wish, to send any Athenian citizen into ten years' of exile. To guard against misuse, a large quorum was called for – 6,000 men. Voting was by secret ballot, and a simple majority sufficed to carry the day. Like other features of Cleisthenes' reforms, the device was clearly planned as yet another safeguard against the accumulation of power in the hands of one individual.

In the matter of civic administration, his reforms were no less revolutionary. Noticing, no doubt, the political unreliability of the Assembly, in which citizens voted each on his own and were easily swayed by circumstance into voting the way the powerful and the specious wished, he instituted another body, the so-called 'Council of 500,' to carry on the effective government of the state. This, too, was based upon his new system of ten tribes. Every year each tribe sent to the Council a delegation of fifty members (chosen by lot from citizens over thirty who expressed willingness to stand and were demonstrably eligible to do so). I say "by lot"; I shall be returning later to this remarkable feature of the Athenian system. Each delegation presided in turn for 1/10 of the year (i.e. for approximately five weeks) in fixed rotation, serving as a steering-committee for the whole. As a crowning feature of the system, a President of each of the delegations was appointed daily—again by lot!—and that President who happened to preside over the delegation serving at the time as steering-committee was in fact what we might call 'Prime Minister for the Day.'

All this remarkable, by any norms of egalitarianism, and with these reforms Cleisthenes had undoubtedly laid the basis for Athenian democracy. But it would be a mistake to think that full citizenship-participation was now the order of the day, or that Cleisthenes had any such goal in mind. While great strides towards such participation had been made, important civic posts will remained the prerogative of the privileged. The new Council, for example, in effect took over most of the duties of a long-standing body (the so-called

Areopagus, or Senate) which was populated entirely by members of the two upper-income classes who had held the highest office of state, but the Areopagus still continued in being as a prestigious and influential body. Again, public officials may have been accountable to the Assembly, and so were in that sense clearly accountable to the entire citizen-body, but in practice those who were in a position to fill such posts, which were at that time *unpaid* (and there's the rub), were of course the relatively well-off; so in this area, too, members of the two upper-income classes tended to dominate. Even in the case of the Council, things can hardly have been much different. After all, membership of the Council was a full-time (unpaid) job for a year, with a possible extension for a second. Who but the relatively affluent could afford to run for possible membership? The same can be said of the ten military commanders elected annually from the ten tribes; all the evidence suggests that, with rare exceptions, they too were drawn from the ranks of the well-to-do. When all is said and done, it was probably only in the Assembly at this time that the voice of *all* interested citizens was felt, and that because the Assembly met usually only ten times a year (this was later raised to forty), and attendance at the handful of important-looking meetings would not unduly interfere with the business of earning a living. And all this may very well have been as Cleisthenes intended it. From what evidence there is, it seems very likely that he had in mind two major objectives: first, a society free from the possibility of future subversion of powerful individuals or factions (in this, he was brilliantly successful), and secondly, a society where every official was ultimately accountable to the whole people in Assembly. What he did *not* apparently plan—and if he planned, did not succeed in attaining—was full citizenship-participation in the day-to-day running of the community. The nearest this came to happening was after the year 462, after reforms associated with the names of Ephialtes and Pericles. At this time the old Areopagus was effectively abolished, and its remaining powers transferred to the Council and Assembly. Perhaps more importantly, a modest daily *payment* was now offered for jury-service, and as time went on a nominal fee was also offered for service on the Council and in a number of other civic posts, and eventually even for attendance at the Assembly.

How all this worked out in practice is best understood, I think, by means of an imaginary scenario. Suppose the year is, say, 417 B.C. You are forty-five years of age, and live in the city of Athens. What would the chances be of your public participation in the city's life—assuming that you felt an inclination to serve? Well, that would depend on a number of things. If you were a forty-five year old *slave* (male or female) you would be *ipso facto* excluded from *any* say in the running of the city; slaves were not citizens. If you were a forty-five year old *woman* (albeit a free one), you would be similarly excluded; public life was the prerogative of free adult males only. Suppose you were a forty-five year old 'resident alien', as they were called? You had learned the trade of potter in, say, Corinth, and had come to Athens to live. Because, however, both your *parents* were not Athenian citizens, you were forever excluded from the right of Athenian citizenship, and consequently forever excluded from active participation in the city's political life.

Imagine now a forty-five year old *citizen*, who has been able to show, under public scrutiny, that he is in all respects fully eligible to participate in public life. He also happens to belong to the *lowest* of the four property-classes. So the chances are that he will spend some of his time attending the Assembly; I say 'some', because at this time no fee is offered for attendance (that will come later) and he can't afford to spend too much of his time away from the business of earning a living. He turns up usually on the occasions when the agenda looks interesting, or when the ten generals have called a special meeting, usually involving matters of peace or war. In cases other than the latter, the business to be discussed will come directly from the Council, and will carry the Council's recommendations; but it is the Assembly that debates the matter and makes the final decision. Whatever old Cleisthenes may have intended, it is not in the Council, but in the Assembly that the *major* decisions of state are taken, and *his* vote counts there; so he tries to be around on the big occasions. He remembers with mixed feelings how his grandfather cast his vote in the Assembly years ago when Themistocles was ostracised; how his father was in the Assembly in 431 when Athens cast its vote in favour of war with Sparta. This year he himself is present in the Assembly, and the feeling of sheer power that his citizenship bestows on him has never felt stronger. A spell-binding speaker, Hyperbolus, counting too easily on the support of the Assembly (which had been very much behind him up to now), has over-reached himself in trying to ostracise Alcibiades and got *himself* ostracised instead! And our citizen's vote figured in the decision. He *floats* home in the evening. . . .

Imagine now a sixty-one year old equally low-income citizen (why I say sixty-one will become clear shortly) who has been able to show that he is in no way disbarred from participating in public life. The chances are he will spend a good deal of his time serving in the extensive jury-system. 6000 such jurors were empanelled to serve every year, and out of an entire citizen-body of about 21,000, some 10,000 of the most able-bodied would be tied up in military service abroad, garrison-duties, and the like. So the panel of 6,000 jurors would be drawn from a group of male citizens of perhaps only twice that number, most of them past the age of military service (which in Athens meant past the age of sixty); which means that our low-income senior citizen would stand an even chance of selection to the panel, were he to express an interest in standing. Equally importantly—*he* could *afford* to be on jury-call for a year in a way that younger members of his prop-erty-class could not; his state pension plus the jury-fee would keep *him* in relative comfort, but hardly *them*. How *much* jury-service he would actually see would be a matter of luck, however, since selection to serve on a particular jury was drawn from the eligible 6,000 names—you guessed it!—by lot.

As an example of the sort of trial he might have attended, I have chosen some excerpts from a trial of a couple of genera-tions later of which the main speech of the prosecutor has survived. Though it comes from a period in Athens' history slightly later than the one we are discussing, there is no reason for believing that it is not very much the sort of thing that could have taken place then. The back-ground, briefly, is this. The advocate Demosthenes, in conjunction with a prominent politician Timarchus, had brought a treason-charge against the advocate Aeschines. As a counter-attack, and in an attempt to delay the impending trial, Aeschines brought an indictment against one of his prosecutors, Timarchus, declaring that the viciousness of the latter's private life precluded him by law from ever again addressing himself to the Athenian people in the Assembly. While this would not technically have prevented him from still proceeding with his plan to indict Aeschines in the courts, it was certainly likely to do him great damage in the eyes of a *jury* on any such occasion, and this was clearly what Aeschines had in mind by bringing his own pre-emptive indictment.

At this point we can take our place in the court with the jury, and lend an ear to the proceedings. Since this is an Athenian court, Aeschines will be allowed full rein to adduce any argument that he thinks will win him his case. There is no law of libel, for example, to deter him. And there will be no counsel for the defence to spring up periodically with the cry of "Objection!"; no judge to reply "Objection over-ruled", or "Objection sustained." The jury will have to listen to the entire speech without interruption, and then that of the defendant's advocate (who, not surprisingly, turns out to be Demosthenes)—again without interruption. Without guidance of any sort they will have to disentangle for themselves the relevancies from the irrelevancies, the flights of fancy from the hard facts, the valid reasoning from the invalid, the sound from the unsound, and then come up with a majority conclusion, which will decide the issue.

The heart of Aeschines' case is that Timarchus had as a younger man been a male prostitute, and that this by law excludes him from any further participation in Athenian public life, including the proceedings of the Assembly. Aeschines wastes little time getting down to the matter. (He is addressing the Clerk of the Court).

(*To the Clerk*)　Read this law to the jury, that you may know, gentlemen, in the face of what established laws of yours, so good and so moral, Timarchus has had the effrontery to speak before the people—a man whose character is so notorious.

The Law
[If any Athenian shall have prostituted his person, he shall not be permitted to become one of the nine archons; nor to discharge the office of priest, nor to act as an advocate for the state, nor shall he hold any office whatsoever, at home or abroad, whether filled by lot or by election; he shall not take part in debate, nor be present at the public sacrifices; and he shall not enter within the limits of the place that has been purified for the assembling of the people. If any man who has been convicted of prostitution act contrary to these prohibitions, he shall be put to death.]

The law is clear, and if (as seems to have been the case) Timarchus really *had* been a male prostitute, then he had obviously broken it. But Aeschines is not ready to leave it at that. A sober-minded jury of Athenian citizens should know something more about the heinousness of the crime. . . .What is ultimately degrading and unspeakable about male prostitution, he argues, is that its practitioners are (horror of horrors) *women* (!) in their vices, not men; their crime is against nature, and involves the abuse of their own persons. . . .

Such, then, was the judgment of your fathers concerning things shameful and things honourable; and shall their sons let Timarchus go free, a man chargeable with the most shameful practices, a creature with the body of man defiled with the sins of a woman? In that case, who of you will punish a *woman* if he finds her in wrong doing? Or what man will not be regarded as lacking in intelligence who is angry with her who errs by an impulse of nature, while he takes counsel from the man who in despite of nature has abused his own person? How will each man of you feel as he goes home from court? For the person who is on trial is no obscure man, but well known; the law governing the official scrutiny of public speakers is not a trivial law, but a most excellent one; and we must expect that the boys and young men will ask the members of their families how the case was decided. What then, pray, are you going to answer, you in whose hands the decision now rests, when your sons ask you whether you voted for conviction or acquittal? When you acknowledge that you set Timarchus free, will you not at the same time be overturning our whole system of training the youth?

What is worse in the case of Timarchus and some of the people of like profession that Demosthenes will be calling his defence, their clients were often *Athenian citizens*! Such conduct damages the Athenian people. Now had the clients been foreigners, or resident aliens, that would of course have been different. . . .

Before you hear the pleas of these men in his support, call to mind their lives, and bid those who have sinned against their own bodies to cease annoying you and to stop speaking before the people. And as they are hunters of such young men as are easily trapped, command them to turn their attention to the *foreigners* and the *resident aliens*, that they may still indulge their predilection, but without injuring you!

Athens also has strong laws against the sexual abuse of men, women, and children, slave or free.

The law says explicitly: if any boy is let out for hire as a prostitute, prosecution is not to lie against the boy himself, but against the man who let him out for hire and the man who hired him. And the law has made the penalties for both offenders the same. And what other law has been laid down for the protection of your children? The law against panders. For the lawgiver imposes the heaviest penalties if any person act as pander in the case of a free-born child or a free-born woman.

And what other law? The law against sexual abuse, which includes all such conduct in one summary statement.

(*To the Clerk*.)   Read the law.

The Law

[If any Athenian shall sexually abuse a free-born child, the parent or guardian of the child shall prosecute him, and shall demand a specific penalty. If the court condemn the accused to death, he shall be delivered to the constables and be put to death the same day. If he be condemned to pay a fine, and be unable to pay the fine immediately, he must pay within eleven days after the trial, and he shall remain in prison until payment is made. The same action shall hold against those who abuse the persons of slaves.]

Now perhaps some one, on first hearing this law, may wonder for what possible reason this word "slaves" was added in the law against sexual abuse. But if you reflect on the matter, fellow citizens, you will find this to be the best provision of all. For it was not for the slaves that the lawgiver was concerned, but he wished to accustom you to keep a long distance away from the crime of sexually abusing free men, and so he added the prohibition against the sexual abusing even of slaves. In a word, he was convinced that in a democracy that man is unfit for citizenship who sexually abuses any person whatsoever.

What Aeschines has apparently passed over, of course, is the fact that Timarchus does not stand accused of the sexual *abuse* of *anyone*! Or such would seem to be the case on any normal reading of the law. But Aeschines, as we have seen, has his own reading of the law: Timarchus *has* in fact as a prostitute sexually abused someone—he has abused his *own person*!

Other distinctions must also be made, says Aeschines. As a homosexual himself, he has no objections to a steady relationship between two males; it is Timarchus' *promiscuity* that is the trouble. He is also fully aware that Demosthenes plans to bring up the matter of his own (i.e. Aeschines') well-known homosexual affairs and the erotic poems he has occasionally sent to male friends. So he tries to forestall the objections. (The world 'lover' in his remarks means in all cases 'homosexual lover').

> ....I understand Demosthenes is going to carry the war into my territory, and ask me if I am not ashamed on my own part, after having made a nuisance of myself in the gymnasia and having been many times a lover, now to be bringing the practice into reproach and danger. And finally—so I am told—in an attempt to raise a laugh and start silly talk among you, he says he is going to exhibit all the erotic poems I have ever addressed to one person or another, and he promises to call witnesses to certain quarrels and fisticuffs in which I have been involved in consequence of this habit.

> Well, I do not deny that I myself have been a lover and am

a lover to this day, nor do I deny that the jealousies and quarrels that commonly arise from the practice have happened in my case. As to the poems which they say I have composed, some I acknowledge, but as to others I deny that they are of the character that these people will impute to them.

The distinction which I draw is this: to be in love with those who combine beauty with moderation is the experience of a kind-hearted and generous soul; but to hire oneself out for money and to indulge in licentiousness is the act of a man who is wanton and ill-bred. And whereas it is an honour to be the object of a pure love, I declare that he who has played the prostitute by inducement of wages is disgraced....The same lawgiver said, "A *slave* shall not be the lover of a free boy nor follow after him, or else he shall receive fifty blows of the public lash." But the free man was not forbidden to love a boy, and associate with him, and follow after him, nor did the lawgiver think that harm came to the boy thereby, but rather that such a thing was a testimony to the man's self-control. But I think, so long as the boy is not his own master and is as yet unable to discern who is a genuine friend, and who is not, the law teaches the lover self-control, and makes him defer declaration of love till the other is older and has reached years of discretion. . . .

In any case, as everyone knows, Demosthenes himself is of doubtful sexuality!

In the case of Demosthenes, too, it was common report that gave him his nickname; and well did common report name him Batalus, for his effeminacy and unnatural lusts! For, Demosthenes, if anyone should strip off those exquisite, pretty cloaks of yours, and the soft, pretty shirts that you wear while you are writing your speeches against your friends, and should pass them around among the jurors, I think, unless they were informed beforehand, they would be quite at a loss to say whether they had in their hands the clothing of a man or of a woman!

And so on. How Demosthenes replied, or how the members of the jury re-acted individually to Aeschines' combination of self-righteousness, sharp-practice, and irrelevancies, we do not know. One important thing, however, we *do* know: Aeschines won!

Imagine now an adult citizen of forty-five in the same time and place, but this time a member of the 'hoplite' class (which would be something like our 'middle' class). He has seen a lot of rugged military service during his twenties and thirties as a heavy-armed soldier during the Great War (now in its fourteenth year), and even now, like all citizens, is technically liable for call-up till the age of sixty. But the chances of that are considerably less than when he was twenty-five to thirty, and he wishes at this stage in his life to participate more actively in public life than he was able hitherto. He is reasonably well-off, and can afford for a two-year stint to accept the token payment from the state to stand for membership of Council. He does, and is chosen (by lot) as one of the fifty from his tribe for the year 417. As a member of the 500-man Council he will help prepare business for the Assembly, receive all foreign delegations, check the qualifications of Public Officials, administer pensions to senior citizens, supervise public works and the all-important shipping industry, and much more. A full and interesting life, and no doubt its own reward to those committed to public service. It has to be; the pay is nominal. He has only one minor worry; and that is, the possibility that some time during the year the office of 'Prime Minister for a Day' may fall by lot to him. The post is prestigious, of course, but there is one possible snag: the Assembly is a stickler for technicalities, and if under his aegis a motion is put to Council that infringes the letter of the law he is liable to disgrace and a stiff fine. In his darker moments he occasionally finds himself wishing he had less money and standing than he has, and could confine his attention, like the

44

poorest citizens, to the Law Courts and the Assembly, where he could enjoy all the satisfactions of power without responsibility.

Imagine finally an adult citizen of forty-five in the same time and place, but this time a member of the one or two per cent that formed the wealthiest class in Athenian society. Money is no problem, so he feels at liberty to propose his name for membership on the Board of Ten Generals, or for one of several other offices, usually involving war and State Security, that admit of re-appointment. (The majority of other offices of state are chosen by lot, and do *not* admit of re-appointment. For this reason they are of little moment to anyone interested in prestige, power, and a high profile, and can be adequately filled by members of the lower- and middle-income classes.) The Ten Generals are not chosen by lot but *elected* annually by the Assembly, one for each tribe, and can stand for re-election indefinitely. So should he do a good job, and win a reputation for sound statesmanship and/or sound military sense in the eyes of Council and Assembly, he stands his best chance of attaining the maximum power that Athenian democracy will allow the individual to hold. (A supreme example of such a success-story in the previous generation was Pericles.) But he must exercise caution. A job improperly done and he risks prosecution at the end of his term of office (like *all* office-holders in Athens), or worse, ostracism, if he makes enough enemies, or something even worse than that, as I shall be mentioning in my discussion of the Peloponnesian War.

What we are looking at here is the western world's first experiment with democratic institutions. The experiment cannot, I think, be fully assessed until we see how Athens and her institutions coped with the stress of a major war, but a number of interim things can be said. We might begin with a few comments made by the anonymous author of a document called "The Constitution of the Athenians," which from the internal evidence clearly stems from the period we are discussing. The author (known by many as "The Old Oligarch") is an Athenian blue-blood, with no love for the democracy; he is ready to admit, however, that Athens has learned to make democracy work to her advantage. Let us listen to a few of the things he says.

First, a remarkable statement that, however much his good oligarchic heart despises what he calls "the baser folk", it is ultimately *just* that the people who keep Athens going—and in particular those who keep her fleet going (for Athens would die without her sea-power)—should have a major say in her governance.

> Now, as concerning the constitution of the Athenians, and the type of manner of constitution which they have chosen, I praise it not, in so far as the very choice involves the welfare of the baser folk as opposed to that of the better class. I repeat, I withhold my praise so far; but, given the fact that this is the type agreed upon, I propose to show that they set about its preservation in the right way; and that those other transactions in connection with it, which are looked upon as blunders by the rest of the Hellenic world, are the reverse.
>
> In the first place, I maintain, it is only just that the poorer classes and the people of Athens should be better off than the men of birth and wealth, seeing that it is the people who man the fleet, and put round the city her girdle of power. The steersman, the boatswain, the commandant, the lookout-man at the prow, the shipwright—these are the ones who engird the city with power rather than her heavy infantry and men of birth and quality. This being the case, it seems only just that offices of state should be thrown open to every one both in the ballot and the show of hands, and that the right of speech should belong to any one who likes, without restriction.

Such institutions, he goes on, are not only just: they are

also cleverly designed to protect the interest of the majority, whose prime interest is in freedom and mastery of their own fate, not in good government and their own subservience to someone else.

> What it comes to, therefore, is that a state founded upon such institutions will not be the best state; but, given a democracy, these are the right means to secure its preservation. The people, it must be borne in mind, does not demand that the city should be well governed and itself a slave. It desires to be free and to be master. As to bad legislation it does not concern itself about that. In fact, what you believe to be bad legislation is the very source of the people's strength and freedom. But if you seek for good legislation, in the first place you will see the cleverest members of the community laying down the laws for the rest. And in the next place, the better class will curb and chastise the lower orders; the better class will deliberate on behalf of the state, and not suffer crack-brained fellows to sit in council, or to speak or vote in the assembly. No doubt; but under the weight of such blessings the people will in a very short time be reduced to slavery.

The same wisdom is shown in the majority's determination to leave certain sensitive positions in the state-apparatus to what he calls "the more powerful citizens".

> For observe, there are many of these offices which, according as they are in good or in bad hands, are a source of safety or of danger to the people, and in these the people prudently abstains from sharing; as, for instance, it does not think it incumbent on itself to share in the functions of the general or of the commander of cavalry. The sovereign people recognizes the fact that in forgoing the personal exercise of these offices, and leaving them to the control of the more powerful citizens, it secures the balance of advantage to itself. It is only those departments of government which bring emolument and assist the private estate that the people cares to keep in its own hands.

As for Athens' treatment of her slaves and resident aliens, this too he says works to Athens' advantage, though it might be considered a source of grave weakness in any other society, such as Sparta.

> Another point is the extraordinary amount of license granted to slaves and resident aliens at Athens, where a blow is illegal, and a slave will not step aside to let you pass him in the street. I will explain the reason of this peculiar custom. Supposing it were legal for a slave to be beaten by a free citizen, or for a resident alien or freedman to be beaten by a citizen, it would frequently happen that an Athenian might be mistaken for a slave or an alien and receive a beating; since the Athenian people is not better clothed than the slave or alien, nor in personal appearance is there any superiority.

If we leave aside for the moment the Old Oligarch's own prejudices in favour of what he calls "the better class" (i.e. himself and friends) and against just about everyone else in Athenian society, his basic statement is remarkable, and all the more worthy of credence, it seems, because it is wrenched grudgingly from a hostile critic, rather than intoned for our edification by some 'true believer.' But credence should be tempered with caution. 'Democracy' is notoriously one of those buzz-words that is used nowadays without a blush by members of every shade of the political spectrum, and we must look a little more precisely at just what this 'people' consists in that is supposed to exercise power, and just what the nature of the power is. Some hints of the situation you will have already gathered from my earlier scenario for the year 417. The Athenian people consisted of all citizens of Athens and surrounding countryside (called Attica); at the height of Athens' prosperity this number has been variously estimated at about between 30,000 and 60,000 men. You will notice that I say 'men'; when Athenians talked about citizens they could on occasion be referring to women and children, as well as men; but more often than not they were speaking fairly strictly of those eligible to participate in the political life of the city, and these consisted of adult *males* who could prove birth from Athenian parents, met the required property-qualifications, and were not in any other way formally disbarred from such participation. (The profile of women in Athenian society was, with rare exceptions, a low one, as is no doubt starting to become clear.) In addition to the citizens there were the 'metics', or 'resident aliens'; their numbers at any one time are hard to estimate. But they were a significant section of the population, and contributed by their skills in a major way to the cultural, commercial and artistic life of the city. We know that on the piece-work involved in the building of the Erechtheum, for example, metics out-numbered citizens by three to one. For the duration of their stay – which was frequently decades for immigrants and a life-time in the case of their children – they remained (with rare exceptions) non-citizens, were forbidden (with rare exceptions) to buy land, and had no formal say in the conduct of Athens' political affairs. They were, however, subject to taxation (though admittedly this constituted a fairly small sum) and military service; there are frequent references to their helping man warships, for example, or serving in the heavy infantry.

And then, of course, there was the slave-population. Their numbers it is impossible to be sure of, but one fairly recent estimate puts the figure at about 80,000 to 100,000 at the time of Athens' greatest power. This would make it approximately 1 1/2 for each Athenian citizen in the stricter sense (i.e. each adult male eligible for participation in political life) or one in four of the whole population. They were mainly employed, it seems, in domestic service, and were owned by people ranging from the very rich (like Nicias, the military commander, who apparently owned 1,000), to those of fairly modest means (if the evidence of Aristophanes does not deceive us); the poorest citizens of all, however, do not appear to have had them. Where they came from varied: some had been captured in war, some imported from the slave-markets of Asia Minor and elsewhere, others were slaves because their parents were. What characterized them *all*, whatever their origins, was their chattel-status. Having said that, I must go on to make a few distinctions. To begin with, a significant number (perhaps even the majority) of Athenian slaves worked *alongside* their masters; they were an extra pair of hands to help bake the bread, weave clothing, hoe the land, bring in the harvest; it is wholly misleading to think of them as a class of toilers working for masters who would not have understood what it was to do a day's work of their own. Their basic 'servitude' consisted of the fact that, in addition to their chattel status, they were usually unpaid for their labour or, if they *were* paid, saw their wage handed over to their master, whose profit lay in the difference between that wage and the slave's upkeep. I say 'usually', because certain slaves were allowed to "live apart", as the saying went, to work on their own at their own trade, paying part of their earnings to their master and keeping the rest. A few of these clearly went on to become independently wealthy and eventually even buy their own release, and this is what among other things made our fastidious Old Oligarch so unhappy. Another point that bothered him, you will remember, was Athens' apparent determination to make life a reasonably tolerable one for its slaves, to guarantee them legal redress against abusive treatment, and in general to minimize the differences between slave and free in daily life and dress. In this respect, as we shall see, Athenian slaves were all-in-all far better treated than their counterparts in, say, Sparta. The only possible exception to this rule were the slaves who worked in groups in back-breaking jobs like the silver mines of Laurium. During the ten-year period, for example, that the Spartans occupied Decelea during the Peloponnesian War we know that 20,000 slaves took the chance to run, and a significant number of these we can be sure were toilers in the silver mines.

To return now to the question I posed a short while ago: the 'people' that could exercise active political power in Athens consisted it seems of about 1/4 of the total population. The nature of that power, and a possible *rationale* for it, was in part described by the Old Oligarch. For another view (which will conclude this interim account) we can turn to one of Athens' most famous and flamboyant products, Alcibiades, who, if Thucydides is reporting with verbal exactitude, once described Athenian democracy as "acknowledged insanity " (Thuc. 6.89.6). He did not, however, go on to give any precise reason for the statement, and it so happens that at the time he made it he knew that he had done enough damage to Athens' interests to risk trial and death for treason should he ever return there. So we should perhaps treat his statement as colourful, but not wholly unbiassed. Events later proved, nonetheless, that Alcibiades was far from the only one in Athens who believed that the form of democracy espoused by her was more egalitarian than efficient. The lot-system in particular received a good deal of internal criticism (not least from the philosopher Socrates), and it is of course very easy to ridicule. To anyone interested in society's use of the best available talent, it does seem on the face of it absurd that a pivotal body like the Council should be populated by 500 men, every one of whom got there by having his name drawn from a hat; or that the majority of official civic posts should be allotted by the same method. To anyone interested further-more in the efficiency which stems (sometimes at any rate!) from an ongoing body of experience, it may well seem an act of political dementedness on Athens' part that she allowed a citizen at most a stint of two years on the Council and *one year only* in the majority of civic posts. As for her determination to leave major political and military decisions to the majority vote of as many citizens as happened to turn up to the Assembly on a given occasion, their claim to such power based on citizenship rather than any expertise, one might be forgiven for thinking that a city that so conducted its affairs, particularly in time of war, was driven by a death-instinct. All these things can be and have been said, and much more, and will clearly have to be taken into consideration when we come to a fuller assessment of Athenian democracy.

For the moment, however, I should like to leave this topic in abeyance and turn briefly to Athens' major rival, Sparta, and see the lines along which *she* had developed. The account will be necessarily somewhat impressionistic, as our evidence for Sparta's affairs is far slighter, and far more confused, than is our evidence for matters Athenian. The Spartans were of Dorian descent, and settled in the southern Peloponnese, in the valley of the Eurotas. They displaced, and it seems very likely reduced to slavery, the local Laconian inhabitants, who from that time onwards were known as 'Helots' (a word which may stem from the word Helos, one of the Laconian towns that was destroyed, or from the verb for 'to capture'). Unlike other Greek states, the Spartans coped with their expanding population by annexation rather than colonization, and in the eighth century we find them taking over the neighboring state of Messenia and reducing *its* inhabitants too to Helot-status, like the inhabitants of Laconia earlier on. But holding a complete population in serfdom can have been no easy task without the taking of drastic measures; we know, for example, of a long-drawn-out revolt by the Messenians in the seventh century that they must have had great difficulty in suppressing. So several scholars have inferred that it must have been about this time that the socio-political system and the regime of parsimonious and Stoical self-discipline were instituted that have made the name 'Spartan' a by-word even to the present day.

We can begin by discussing the role and status of the least advantaged class, the Helots. The first thing to realize is that they greatly outnumbered the Spartans, by what seems to have been at least five to one and very probably more. They were the possession of the Spartan state, so could not (like Athenian slaves) be bought and sold by individuals. They were, rather, tied to the soil, paying half their crop to the State and retaining the rest for themselves. As a subject-population they were a constant source of worry to the Spartans, who made certain that in time of a war all the adult males accompanied the army as batmen and transporters of equipment. At the battle of Plataea, for example, in 479, we know that the Spartans numbered 5,000 and their Helot attendants 35,000! As the fifth century progressed, and the manpower needs of the Spartan army increased, we hear of Helots volunteering to join the army, and being freed from slavery for their pains. Their title was thenceforth New Citizens, but they do not appear to have enjoyed significant political rights at home; we nearly always find them serving in distant posts overseas, where they are out of sight if not wholly out of mind.

If we are to believe the ancient sources, the Helots were subjected to extraordinarily callous treatment by Sparta. For example, according to Plutarch, the Spartan state officially declared war on them every year, so that no Spartan could be guilty of 'religious impurity' for having killed one of them. According to the same source, the Spartans had an institution called the *Krypteia* or 'Hiding Game', according to which young Spartan warriors were sent out into the countryside equipped only with a dagger and basic rations, on the expectation that they would successfully hide in the day and rub out one or two dangerous-looking Helots by night. Plato, a well-known admirer of Spartan institutions, refused to believe the story, but it would not have been the first or last time in history that self-styled master-races have treated man-hunting of the *Untermensch* as some sort of sport. Whatever the truth in the case of Sparta, we know enough from other sources to be sure that the Helot, tied to the land and without rights, protection, or participation of any sort in civic life, was as far removed in role and status from a Spartan citizen as an ox or donkey is from its owner.

A second group, the so-called '*Perioeci*' ('Dwellers round-about') were considerably better off. These were people who lived in the smaller towns and villages surrounding Sparta. Unlike the Helots, they were racially similar if not identical to the Spartans. Perhaps because of this they enjoyed near-total autonomy in the running of their internal affairs, and their lands were largely their own, except for a number of choice tracts owned by the Spartans, and for which they paid rent. Foreign policy, however, was dictated by Sparta, in whose army they were also compelled to serve. Like the Helots, they always outnumbered their Spartan overlords (though less drastically), and like the Helots had no say in Sparta's political life. Unlike the Helots, they seem to have been reasonably content with their lot, or at least resigned to it; at any rate we seldom hear of any revolts.

The third and final group consists of the Spartans themselves. At their head were two hereditary kings (two, presumably, as a check on potential autocratic power-grabbing). From about the turn of the fifth century, the point was reinforced by a regulation that only one of the kings be allowed at any one time to leave the city for purposes of waging a war. This king was chosen to conduct the war by an Assembly (membership of which consisted, like its Athenian counterpart, of the entire citizen-body), and war was declared by (and only by) that Assembly.

At home, the two kings were merely two among a group of thirty called the 'Council of Elders'. This body consisted of male citizens aged sixty or over, who were elected for life by public acclamation of all the citizens in Assembly. As far as we know, no qualification of property or birth was required: all senior citizens were eligible to stand as candidates. The exact degree of the Council's power and influence is rather difficult to gauge, but we *do* know that it served as Sparta's criminal court, and in particular judged all cases involving the death penalty—including, significantly, impeachment of the kings.

This brings us to the Assembly, a body which, like its Athenian counterpart, consisted of all Spartan males above the age of thirty who had not defaulted in their military and disciplinary duties. We have already seen some of its powers, to which should be added its right to elect annually a board of five magistrates, called Ephors, to serve its interests. Cicero compares them, not without some justification, to the 'tribunes of the people' in his own Republican Rome. None could hold office twice, and policy on any occasion was decided by majority-vote among them. Their power was very extensive—on the domestic front far surpassing that of the two kings, for example. They had among other things powers of arrest and punishment over all citizens, including the kings. According to one source, one of the kings, Archidemus, was once fined by them for marrying a short wife. Their reason? "She will bear us, not kings, but kinglets!"

To complete the picture, we must say a word about that feature of the system which is perhaps best known: the military discipline. We have already seen how the serf-population greatly outnumbered their Spartan masters, and it comes as little surprise to find the Spartans much concerned to preserve themselves and the system by making of themselves an invincible military machine. They had, of course, the leisure-time to do this; unlike their Athenian counterparts, they left their land to be looked after almost entirely by the Helots, thus liberating themselves for other things. If our ancient authorities are to be our guide, those "other things" began at birth, when the decision whether to preserve or destroy the child lay, not with the parents, but the State authorities. If the child was physically strong, it was preserved; if not, it was thrown over a cliff. Training for a boy began at the age of seven or eight, and from the ages of fourteen to twenty he was enrolled in what was called a 'herd', under the close supervision of one of the older youths and the more general supervision of one of the older State authorities specifically appointed to the task. The training he went through was mainly athletic and military, and seems to have been uncompromisingly tough and brutal. Living was communal, and rations were meagre, and we hear among other things how the stealing of food to supplement them was encouraged, with punishment for those so clumsy as to get caught. Xenophon the historian, a well-known admirer of Sparta, has the following to say (the 'he' is the Spartan law-giver Lycurgus):

> It is obvious that the whole of this education tended, and was intended, to make the boys craftier and more inventive in getting supplies, while at the same time it cultivated their warlike instincts. An objector may retort: "But if he thought it so fine a feat to steal, why did he inflict all those blows on the unfortunate who was caught?" My answer is: for the selfsame reason which induces people, in other matters which are taught, to punish the malperformance of a service. So they, the Spartans, visit penalties on the boy who is detected thieving as being but a sorry bungler in the art.

At the age of twenty the young man was admitted to the army and became eligible to join a *sussition*, which was a military-style dining club or mess-hall which according to Plutarch averaged about fifteen members, but may in fact have been considerably more than that. This is where he ate every day for the rest of his fighting life, his meals consisting for the most part of a substantial but monotonous diet of barley, wine, cheese, figs, and a main course of what seems to have been a form of haggis. He continued to live in a dormitory, and if he married, could only visit his wife secretly, and then return to the dormitory; only later (perhaps after the first child was born) was he allowed to set up house with her. Military training was the central and ongoing part of his life, and all facets of his existence indicated the final goal: the production of the single-minded, simple-living, superbly disciplined soldier. In addition to the discipline I have been talking about, the Spartan was also forbidden to possess all except iron coinage (which was usable only in Spartan territory, thus effectively making the buying of dangerous, foreign luxury-goods impossible) and was restricted by sumptuary laws to putting up a house of the barest simplicity. Here is Xenophon again:

> There are yet other customs in Sparta which Lykourgos instituted in opposition to those of the rest of Hellas, among them the following. We all know that in the other states every one makes as much money as he can—one man as a tiller of the soil, another as a mariner, a third as a merchant, while others depend on various arts to earn a living. But at Sparta Lykourgos forbade his freeborn citizens to have anything whatsoever to do with the concerns of money-making. As freemen, he enjoined upon them to regard as their concern exclusively those activities upon which the foundations of civic liberty are based.

> He went a step further and set up a strong barrier. . .against the pursuance of money-making by wrongful means. In the first place, he established a coinage of so extraordinary a sort that even a sum of ten minas could not come into a house

without attracting the notice of the master himself or of some member of his household: in fact, it would occupy a considerable space, and need a wagon to carry it. Gold and silver, moreover, are liable to search, and if any is found anywhere the possessor is fined. Indeed,...for what reason should money-making become an earnest pursuit in a community where the possession of wealth entails more pain than its employment brings satisfaction?

Lastly, and most importantly, the Spartan citizen was also under pressure to keep up his payments (in kind) to his mess-hall. Should he default, he risked the loss of his citizenship, and according to one source the ultimate humiliation of demotion to a group of un-persons known as "the Inferiors."

As I have pictured it, life in Sparta was a grim and dour one, not to say a terrifying one at times for at any rate some of the citizens and the ultimate in human bondage for the Helots. Yet we know that some of Athens' most famous sons, including the historian Xenophon and the philosopher Plato, were great admirers of much of the Spartan system, and in many respects clearly preferred it to their own. An attempt to find out why will be part and parcel of a general attempt I shall later be making to assess the merits and demerits of the Spartan vis-à-vis the Athenian system. Neither system, however, it seems to me, can be assessed with complete fairness until we see it operating under stress, and in particular the stress of war. In my next lecture I shall discuss just such a situation—the Peloponnesian War—and how the institutions of both societies stood up to the test.

3 War, and the Lessons of War

In the previous lecture I discussed the socio-political framework of two societies, Athens and Sparta, and I concluded with the observation that a balanced evaluation of their systems could only be made when we had observed both societies under stress—particularly the stress of war. In this lecture I wish to discuss the Great War which the two societies eventually—perhaps even inevitably—fought, with a view to making such an evaluation.

A brief word on the background to the War. The first thing that should be mentioned is a war of fifty years earlier fought by both societies not against each other but against a common enemy, Persia. On two occasions Persia invaded Greece with massive forces, and on both occasions was decisively defeated. On the first occasion, in 490, she was defeated at Marathon by a force consisting largely of Athenians; Sparta was busy celebrating a religious festival, and arrived the day after it was all over. But the danger was not yet over, and a second invasion loomed. An Athenian commander of distinction had emerged in Themistocles, and at his urging the Athenians used the income from a recently discovered lode in the Laurium silver mines to enlarge their tiny fleet to a massive one consisting of 200 warships. (The implications of this, not just for the upcoming battle with the Persians—and for that matter with her next-door neighbour, the formidable sea-power Aegina—but for Athens' entire future history, will soon be apparent.) The second invasion came, under the command of Xerxes, and both Athens and Sparta enhanced their reputations when it was repulsed. Sparta on land, and Athens both on land and at sea, had performed heroically in military engagements that have gone down in history: Thermopylae, Artemisium, Salamis, Plataea. But with the common danger past, the two powers went their separate ways. As elected leader of the Greek forces against Xerxes, Sparta might have been expected to use its enhanced reputation as a military force to seek to widen its sphere of domination within Greece once the war was over. But her physical losses had been heavy, and she preferred to return to the Peloponnese to head what she hoped would be a more manageable body of states there that became known as the Spartan Alliance.

Athens meanwhile had been left free to use her newly acquired fleet to continue the war against Persia—and in particular to liberate those Greek cities on the Ionian seaboard that were under Persia's control, and to protect the many island states between her and Ionia that would be the first to fall under Persia's control were she to attack again and be successful. Under such circumstances she had little difficulty forming an alliance with these maritime and island-states. Her position was (in theory, at any rate) that of 'first among equals'; as such, she was the guarantor of the independence of each state. She commanded the combined navies, and assessed the contributions (either in money or ships) that each state would make to the Alliance.

By the middle of the fifth century, however, things had started to go sour, and Athens stood accused of exploitation and imperialism. A number of the allied states had revolted from her, and for their pains had lost their navies and their independence; from now on they were forced to pay Athens annual tribute (rather than 'contributions'). An even larger number had from an early date decided (with or without a little persuasion) to make cash contributions to the Alliance, rather than ships and men, and these watched in anger and frustration as they saw Athens' own sea-power grow to near-invincible proportions as a result. And there were further aggravations. Some at any rate of their money the allied states could see was being diverted into the embellishment of Athens itself, and they resented such things as Athens' demand of an oath of loyalty to her; or the fact that major court cases were to be heard only in Athens; or the presence, in certain states, of Athenian military garrisons; or the tell-tale fact that in 454 the central treasury of the Alliance was moved from the sacred island of Delos to Athens itself. The high-handed tone of this decree concerning Erythrae gives some idea of what many of the allied states must have found galling:

> Erythrae shall have a council of 120 men chosen by lot. The council shall examine (the qualifications of) each man so chosen: an alien may not be a councilor, nor anyone under 30 years of age, and violators (of this provision) shall be liable to prosecution. No one shall be a councilor twice within four years. The present council shall be drawn by lot and constituted by the (Athenian) overseers and garrison commander, in future by the council itself and the commander not less than thirty days before the council goes out of office. They shall swear by Zeus, Apollo and Demeter, imprecating utter destruction upon those who swear false and utter destruction upon their children. . . .

> The council oath is as follows: "To the best and truest of my ability I will serve as councilor for the people of Erythrai and Athens and the allies. I will not revolt against the people of Athens or against the allies of Athens, either of my own accord or at the behest of another, and I will not defect, either of my own accord or at the behest of any other person at all."

While alarmed at the growth of Athens' naval empire,

Sparta was in the early years much too preoccupied with disaffection within its own Spartan Alliance to do much about it, and matters were not helped when the thing that all Spartans feared happened—the Helots of Messenia rose up in revolt against their masters in 469, and in 464 the local Laconian Helots did likewise, joining the rebels entrenched at Ithome. Sparta's situation was desperate, and one wonders what might have happened had not Athens and a few lesser states decided to come to her aid; as it was, it was 460 before the Helots capitulated. From this point on she could turn at any rate some of her attention to Athens, but as a land power could do little to stop the growth and consolidation of Athens' sea-empire. An armistice between the two was finally concluded in 451, to last till 446, and from that date we have an uneasy peace till the outbreak of the Great War in 431.

As I mentioned earlier, I plan to talk about this war with a particular goal in mind: that is, to discover in what way the two contending socio-political systems and ideologies made it what it was and how each stood up to the test it imposed on them. As a framework for such a discussion one can briefly sum up the conflict as follows: for twenty-seven years (with one very brief interlude) two powerful states were locked in combat. The reasons for the length of the war are no doubt many, but two stand out: the depth of the ideological differences between the two contenders, and the fact that each found it difficult to get a stranglehold on the other, since one was basically a land-power and the other basically a sea-power. The situation has been compared to a fight between an elephant and a whale. Sparta, with next to no navy, could not seriously disrupt sea-borne supplies to Athens; Athens in turn did not have land-forces powerful enough to take on Sparta. Each side posted a number of victories and defeats in the early years, none of them amounting to a knockout blow, and in 415, sixteen years after the War began, Athens made an ambitious attempt to end it all by invading Sicily, a major source of Sparta's food-supply. The attempt ended in total failure and crippling losses in men and ships. Athens rebuilt her fleet and struggled on doggedly till 404, when the Spartans and their allies joined forces with the old enemy, Persia, to get control of the Hellespont and block Athens' own food supplies from her colonies on the Black Sea. Hoist with her own petard, Athens surrendered.

An observer of the entire conflict was the historian Thucydides, and his history of the events (from the beginning till the year 411, where it breaks off uncompleted) is universally acknowledged to be one of the masterpieces of Western thought. I plan to use him extensively, not least because his aims in writing the account at least partially coincide with the objective of this particular lecture. This being the case, I shall mention at the outset what seem to me the major biasses of the account, in the hope that as the tale unfolds appreciation for his great brooding genius will be tempered with a quiet dose of caution and critical scepticism.

His background, like that of so many of the writers Athens produced, was aristocratic, and he does not appear to have had much love for democracy, except perhaps for the time when Athens was effectively governed by a man he admired, Pericles. In his own approving words: "in what was nominally a democracy, power was really in the hands of the first citizen." For the sort of government he pretty clearly *preferred* to Athenian democracy, one has to turn to his account of the oligarchic revolution of 411, which temporarily ousted democracy in Athens. "During the first period of this regime the Athenians appear to have had a better government than ever before, at least in my time. There was a *reasonable and moderate blending of the few and the many*, and it was this, in the first place that made it possible for the city to recover from the bad state into which her affairs had fallen." The crucial phrase here is "a reasonable and moderate blending of the few and the many": that is, democracy is tolerable to the degree that it does not interfere with the governance of the state by those *fitted* to do so.

His own family tradition would no doubt account for much of Thucydides' distaste for democracy as he found it operating in Athens, but his disaffection was no doubt accentuated by the fact that in 424 he was banished for life by the Athenians (he was one of the Athenian generals at the time Amphipolis fell to the Spartans)—an enforced leisure period which, as he puts it drily, "gave me rather exceptional facilities for looking into things." As for his other idiosyncrasies and commitments as a historian and philosopher of history, he describes them with disarming candour at the beginning of his book:

> In this history I have made use of set speeches some of which were delivered just before and others during the war. I have found it difficult to remember the precise words used in the speeches which I listened to myself, and my various informants have experienced the same difficulty; so my method has been, while keeping as closely as possible to the general sense of the words that were actually used, to make the speakers say what, in my opinion, was called for by each situation. . .
>
> . . .with regard to my factual reporting of the events of the war I have made it a principle not to write down the first story that came my way, and not even to be guided by my own general impressions; either I was present myself at the events which I have described or else I heard of them from eyewitnesses whose reports I have checked with as much thoroughness as possible. Not that even so the truth was easy to discover: different eye-witnesses give different accounts of the same events, speaking out of partiality for one side or the

other or else from imperfect memories. And it may well be that my history will seem less easy to read because of the absence in it of a romantic element. It will be enough for me, however, if these words of mine are judged useful by those who want to understand clearly the events which happened in the past and which (human nature being what it is) will, at some time or other and in much the same ways, be repeated in the future. My work is not a piece of writing designed to meet the taste of an immediate public, but was done to last for ever.

It is clear from this that the speeches which have done so much to make his book famous will have to be taken as at best impressionistic; and one will also have to keep constantly in mind that Thucydides has three specific beliefs that cannot help but colour the entire account: first, human nature does not change; secondly, history tends to repeat itself in fairly similar patterns; and thirdly, as a consequence, his own book will be of permanent value—presumably elucidatory and predictive value.

Let us turn now to the war itself. We might begin by noting what each side had going for it. Athens had an extensive naval empire, with massive resources in home and allied ships and manpower, formidable reserves of capital, and a near-impregnable food supply route from the Black Sea to its home port, the Piraeus. Sparta headed a formidable league of Peloponnesian states and a few outside the Peloponnese, had a reputation for near-invincibility in battle, and could count on the support of an enormous number of Greeks, not least the frequently affluent and powerful oligarchic factions of supposed Athenian allies like Erythrae who had had democratic constitutions thrust upon them. The rallying cry was 'liberty!':

People's feelings were generally very much on the side of the Spartans, especially as they proclaimed that their aim was the liberation of Hellas. States and individuals alike were enthusiastic to support them in every possible way, both in speech and action, and everyone thought that unless he took a personal share in things the whole effort was being handicapped. So bitter was the general feeling against Athens, whether from those who wished to escape from her rule or from those who feared that they would come under it.

If Sparta had the advantage of a *cause*, Athens had the advantage of possessing at the outbreak of war a singularly resourceful and brilliant leader, Pericles, who in Thucydides' view could undoubtedly have won the war for them, had his advice been faithfully followed:

> Indeed, during the whole period of peace-time when Pericles was at the head of affairs the state was wisely led and firmly guarded, and it was under him that Athens was at her greatest. And when the war broke out, here, too, he appears to have accurately estimated what the power of Athens was. He survived the outbreak of war by two years and six months, and after his death his foresight with regard to the war became even more evident. For Pericles had said that Athens would be victorious if she bided her time and took care of her navy, if she avoided trying to add to the empire during the course of the war, and if she did nothing to risk the safety of the city itself.

Mention of 'risking the city's safety' brings us to a feature of Athenian democracy that Thucydides clearly considered one of a number of reasons for her ultimate discomfiture, but it is interesting to see how to some of her enemies such features were a source of alarm, envy and admiration. Here are some excerpts from a speech that he puts into the mouth of a Corinthian delegate to Sparta just before the outbreak of war. In urging the Spartans to declare war on Athens, he contrasts the dull, conservative, and ultra-cautious ways of Spartans with the mercurial, risk-taking brilliance of Athenians:

An Athenian is always an innovator, quick to form a resolution and quick at carrying it out. You, on the other hand, are good at keeping things as they are; you never originate an idea, and your action tends to stop short of its aim. Then again, Athenian daring will outrun its own resources; they will take risks against their better judgement, and still, in the midst of danger, remain confident. But your nature is always to do less than you could have done, to mistrust your own judgement, however sound it may be, and to assume that dangers will last for ever. Think of this, too: while you are hanging back, they never hesitate; while you stay at home, they are always abroad; for they think that the farther they go the more they will get, while you think that any movement may endanger what you have already. If they win a victory, they follow it up at once, and if they suffer a defeat, they scarcely fall back at all. As for their bodies, they regard them as expendable for their city's sake, as though they were not their own; but each man cultivates his own intelligence, again with a view to doing something notable for his city. If they aim at something and do not get it, they think that they have been deprived of what belonged to them already; whereas, if their enterprise is successful, they regard that success as nothing compared to what they will do next. Suppose they fail in some undertaking; they make good the loss immediately by setting their hopes in some other direction. Of them alone it may be said that they possess a thing almost as soon as they have begun to desire it, so quickly with them does action follow upon decision. And so they go on working away in hardship and danger all the days of their lives, seldom enjoying their possessions because they are always adding to them. Their view of a holiday is to do what needs doing; they prefer hardship and activity to peace and quiet. In a word, they are by nature incapable of either living a quiet life themselves or of allowing anyone else to do so.

Though Thucydides does not spell the matter out in detail, I am myself prepared to believe that he himself believed that such characteristics were *both* Athens' great claim to fame *and* a cause of their ruin in time of war. The same, I think, can be said of a number of features credited to Athens by Pericles in a famous speech at the public funeral of the Athenian war-dead during the winter of the first year of the war. According to Pericles, the difference between the two societies is, briefly, that Sparta is closed in her institutions, and Athens open; Athenians, thanks to democracy, are individually well-informed in their decision-making, the Spartans not. Athenians moreover have a bold and adventurous spirit (the Corinthian delegate said the same thing, it will be recalled), and it is this that underlies their successful acquisition of so great an empire:

> Our city is open to the world, and we have no periodical deportations in order to prevent people observing or finding out secrets which might be of military advantage to the enemy. This is because we rely, not on secret weapons, but on our own real courage and loyalty. There is a difference, too, in our educational systems. The Spartans, from their earliest boyhood, are submitted to the most laborious training in courage; we pass our lives without all these restrictions, and yet are just as ready to face the same dangers as they are. . . .

> Our love of what is beautiful does not lead to extravagance; our love of the things of the mind does not make us soft. We regard wealth as something to be properly used, rather than as something to boast about. As for poverty, no one need be ashamed to admit it: the real shame is in not taking practical measures to escape from it. Here each individual is interested not only in his own affairs but in the affairs of the state as well: even those who are mostly occupied with with own business are extremely well-informed on general politics—this is a peculiarity of ours: we do not say that a man who takes no interest in politics is a man who minds his own business; we say that he has no business here at all. . . .

> . . .Taking everything together then, I declare that our city is an education to Greece, and I declare that in my opinion

each single one of our citizens, in all the manifold aspects of life, is able to show himself the rightful lord and owner of his own person, and does this, moreover, with exceptional grace and exceptional versatility. And to show that this is no empty boasting for the present occasion, but real tangible fact, you have only to consider the power which our city possesses and which has been won by those very qualities which I have mentioned. Athens, alone of the states we know, comes to her testing time in a greatness that surpasses what was imagined of her. In her case, and in her case alone, no invading enemy is ashamed at being defeated, and no subject can complain of being governed by people unfit for their responsibilities. Mighty indeed are the marks and monuments of our empire which we have left. Future ages will wonder at us, as the present age wonders at us now. . . .For our adventurous spirit has forced an entry into every sea and into every land; and everywhere we have left behind us everlasting memorials of good done to our friends or suffering inflicted on our enemies.

Thucydides, typically, offers no comment on the speech, but I for one catch a whiff of *hybris* in the air, and Zeus glancing over towards his stock of thunderbolts.

Let us turn now to the other side of the balance-sheet. What, in Thucydides' view, were the major problems presented to each side by their own socio-political institutions? In the case of Sparta, perhaps the greatest problem was—predictably—how to keep control of their own Helots. One instance of how they dealt with the situation reveals no change in their general ruthlessness in the matter:

They were so frightened of their unyielding character and of their numbers that they had had recourse to the following plan. They made a proclamation to the effect that the helots should choose out of their own number those who claimed to have done the best service to Sparta on the battlefield, implying that they would be given their freedom. This was, however, a test conducted in the belief that the ones who showed most spirit and came forward first to claim their freedom would be the ones most likely to turn against Sparta. So about 2,000 were selected, who put garlands on their heads and went round the temples under the impression that they were being made free men. Soon afterwards, however, the Spartans did away with them, and no one ever knew exactly how each one of them was killed.

Manpower was another problem. The actual number of Spartan troops proper (that is, soldier-citizens, not *perioeci* or Helots) was always very small, and it was this small, tightly knit fighting force that had the reputation of near-invincibility. If *it* ever suffered a serious defeat, Sparta would be in a far worse position than any state suffering a similar defeat, since she would have suffered a major diminution of her citizen-body, the crucial myth of invincibility would have been broken, and considerable encouragement would have been given to Athens and to the Helots. As it happens, this very thing transpired in 425, when a contingent of crack Spartan troops was cut off on the island of Sphacteria and forced to surrender to Athens. Athens received new heart and boldness to continue, and the murmurings of the Helots clearly gave cause for alarm that a revolt was in the offing. Sparta defused the latter problem if not the former by despatching large numbers of Helots out of the country as attendants to an expeditionary army it was sending to Thrace and then dealing with 2,000 of the remainder in the way we have just seen.

What of Athens? Apart from the obvious problem of dealing with a courageous and tenacious enemy, not the least of her problems was dealing with a group of supposed allies, many of whom had revolted from her and had been forced back into the alliance, others of whom grown long since disaffected with her imperial views, and probably all of whom could appreciate, if not fully agree with, Sparta's claim that in this war she was setting out to "liberate them all from slavery." Here is Pericles, in a gem of political candour:

> Then it is right and proper for you to support the imperial dignity of Athens. This is something in which you all take pride, and you cannot continue to enjoy the privileges unless you also shoulder the burdens of empire. And do not imagine that what we are fighting for is simply the question of freedom or slavery: there is also involved the loss of our empire and the dangers arising from the hatred which we have incurred in administering it. Nor is it any longer possible for you to give up this empire, though there may be some people who in a mood of sudden panic and in a spirit of political apathy actually think that this would be a fine and noble thing to do. In fact you now hold your empire down by force: it may have been wrong to take it; it is certainly dangerous to let it go.

At home, small groups of oligarchs, exercising a power far exceeding their numbers, were viewed with fear and distaste by democrats, who saw them (quite rightly, as it turned out) as a potential Spartan fifth-column. Cutting across this division was a further division into what Thucydides calls a 'war-party' and a 'peace-party': a division that became more and more accentuated as the war dragged on. And then there was the inevitable division between those who fought the war and those who made a tidy profit from it. For Thucydides this is all part and parcel of the freedoms of democracy, that may make some sense in peace-time but are ruinous in war:

> Pericles had said that Athens would be victorious if she bided her time and took care of her navy, if she avoided trying to add to the empire during the course of the war, and if she did nothing to risk the safety of the city itself. But his successors did the exact opposite, and in other matters which apparently had no connexion with the war private ambition and private profit led to policies which were bad both for the Athenians themselves and for their allies. Such policies, when successful,

only brought credit and advantage to individuals, and when they failed, the whole war potential of the state was impaired. The reason for this was that Pericles, because of his position, his intelligence, and his known integrity, could respect the liberty of the people and at the same time hold them in check. . . .But his successors, who were more on a level with each other and each of whom aimed at occupying the first place, adopted methods of demagogy which resulted in their losing control over the actual conduct of affairs.

The mention of the word 'demagogy' brings us to the whole question of the role of the Assembly in Athenian policy-making during the war, a matter which Thucydides pretty obviously viewed with a good deal of chagrin, if not disgust. For him the Assembly was only too frequently a forum for political innocents, drunk with the joys of power without responsibility, and too easily misled by the fiery oratory of popular leaders such as Cleon, a fast-talking jingoist with no room for the caution of a Pericles, but a shrewd assessor nonetheless of the same Assembly's flightiness and unreliability as a formulator of war-policy. An example of this can be found in some of the frank things he says to the Assembly in 427–an Assembly which to his annoyance had shown characteristic waywardness and lack of purpose. What had happened, briefly, was this. The island of Mitylene had revolted against Athens, and the Assembly, in an angry mood, had decreed that the entire adult male population of the city be executed, and all women and children enslaved. We can pick up Thucydides' account at that point:

> Next day, however, there was a sudden change of feeling and people began to think how cruel and how unprecedented such a decision was–to destroy not only the guilty, but the entire population of a state. Observing this, the deputation from Mytilene which was in Athens and the Athenians who were supporting them approached the authorities with a view

to having the question debated again. They won their point the more easily because the authorities themselves saw clearly that most of the citizens were wanting someone to give them a chance of reconsidering the matter. So an assembly was called at once. Various opinions were expressed on both sides, and Cleon, the son of Cleaenetus, spoke again. It was he who had been responsible for passing the original motion for putting the Mytilenians to death. He was remarkable among the Athenians for the violence of his character, and at this time he exercised far the greatest influence over the people. He spoke as follows:

'Personally I have had occasion often enough already to observe that a democracy is incapable of governing others, and I am all the more convinced of this when I see how you are now changing your minds about the Mytilenians. Because fear and conspiracy play no part in your daily relations with each other, you imagine that the same thing is true of your allies, and you fail to see that when you allow them to persuade you to make a mistaken decision and when you give way to your own feelings of compassion you are being guilty of a kind of weakness which is dangerous to you and which will not make them love you any more. What you do not realize is that your empire is a dictatorship exercised over subjects who do not like it and who are always plotting against you; you will not make them obey you by injuring your own interests in order to do them a favour; your leadership depends on superior strength and not on any goodwill of theirs. And this is the very worst thing—to pass measures and then not to abide by them. We should realize that a city is better off with bad laws, so long as they remain fixed, than with good laws that are constantly being altered, that lack of learning combined with sound common sense is more helpful than the kind of cleverness that gets out of hand, and that as a general rule states are better governed by the man in the street than by intellectuals.'

Whether Cleon ever put it in those words we don't of course know; but we can be quite sure that that was how

Thucydides viewed both the Assembly and (ironically) Cleon himself. In the present instance the Mitylenians, as it happens, were lucky; the Athenians rejected Cleon's advice second time around, and Thucydides offers a breathtaking account of how the city was saved in the nick of time from destruction. It didn't always work out so fortunately, however, as I shall be mentioning later.

Some final points on the war. The first concerns Truth, war's first casualty, and its bastard cousin, Newspeak. Talking of a common event in the war, in which the democrats of a Spartan-held city would revolt against their oligarchic leaders and call on Athens for help or the oligarchs in an Athenian-held city would overthrow their democrat-rulers and call on Sparta for help, Thucydides describes what he sees as a near-inevitable result of protracted warfare, and something applicable to both sides in any conflict, whatever their original ideals:

> To fit in with the change of events, words, too, had to change their usual meanings. What used to be described as a thought-less act of aggression was now regarded as the courage one would expect to find in a party member; to think of the future and wait was merely another way of saying one was a coward; any idea of moderation was just an attempt to disguise one's unmanly character; ability to understand a question from all sides meant that one was totally unfitted for action. Fanatical enthusiasm was the mark of a real man, and to plot against an enemy behind his back was perfectly legitimate self-defence. Anyone who held violent opinions could always be trusted, and anyone who objected to them became a suspect.

We might look first at a couple of prize pieces of cynicism and verbal gobbledygook on the Spartan side. After two years of siege, the city of Plataea has finally fallen to the Spartans, and the Spartans decide to ask each individual Plataean male a specific question before deciding what to do with him. The question? "Have you done anything to help the Spartans and their allies in the present war?" The Plataeans rightly reply that the question is a cynical *non*-question: if they reply 'No', the penalty is certain death, and if they reply 'Yes', they are manifestly lying, and will suffer the same penalty. The Spartans, unimpressed, put the question anyway, and as each Plataean replied 'No' he was taken away and put to death. All the women were then enslaved.

The second instance concerns a matter purely verbal, but nonetheless I think significant. We have already seen how the Spartans came as what they called 'liberators' from 'Athenian slavery' (one wonders what the Plataean *women* thought of *that* claim?), and the ultimate in Orwellian Newspeak is reached when the Spartans find themselves solemnly talking about the 'involuntary liberation' of cities that have no particular wish to have anything to do with them. Here is the Spartan commander Brasidas, in 424; he has left his army at the gates and entered the city of Acanthus, an ally of Athens, to address the citizens. We pick up his speech as it draws to a close:

> We Spartans are only justified in liberating people against their own will because we are acting for the good of one and all alike. We have no imperialistic ambitions: our whole effort is to put an end to imperialism, and we should be doing wrong to the majority if we were to put up with your opposition to the independence which we are offering to all.

If the Spartan slogan in this war was 'liberation from the oppressor', the Athenian slogan, according to Thucydides, was 'Might is right.' A classic example of its use concerns the little island of Melos. She had managed to maintain something like neutrality throughout the war, but in 416 she was told she must join the Athenian empire or face the consequences. Thucydides describes in gothic detail how the Athenian envoys put their case to the city's rulers, and how the rulers replied. Here are some excerpts from a dialogue that has echoed hauntingly down the centuries:

Athenians:. . .What we shall do now is to show you that it is for the good of our own empire that we are here and that it is for the preservation of your city that we shall say what we are going to say. We do not want any trouble in bringing you into our empire, and we want you to be spared for the good both of yourselves and of ourselves.

Melians: And how could it be just as good for us to be the slaves as for you to be the masters?

Athenians: You, by giving in, would save yourselves from disaster; we, by not destroying you, would be able to profit from you. . .

Melians: So you would not agree to our being neutral, friends instead of enemies, but allies of neither side?

Athenians: No, because it is not so much your hostility that injures us; it is rather the case that, if we were on friendly terms with you, our subjects would regard that as a sign of weakness in us, whereas your hatred is evidence of our power. . .

Melians: Is that your subjects' idea of fair play—that no distinction should be made between people who are quite unconnected with you and people who are mostly your own colonists or else rebels whom you have conquered?

Athenians: So far as right and wrong are concerned they think that there is no difference between the two, that those who still preserve their independence do so because they are strong, and that if we fail to attack them it is because we are afraid. So that by conquering you we shall increase not only the size but the security of our empire. . .We rule the sea and you are islanders, and weaker islanders too than the others; it is therefore particularly important that you should not escape.

Melians: We are not prepared to give up in a short moment the liberty which our city has enjoyed from its foundation for 700 years. We put our trust in the fortune that the gods will send and which has saved us up to now, and in the help of men—that is, of the Spartans; and so we shall try to save ourselves. But we invite you to allow us to be friends of yours and enemies to neither side, to make a treaty which shall be agreeable to both you and us, and so to leave our country.

The Melians made this reply, and the Athenians, just as they were breaking off the discussion, said:

Athenians: Well, at any rate, judging from this decision of yours, you seem to us quite unique in your ability to consider the future as something more certain than what is before your eyes, and to see uncertainties as realities, simply because you would like them to be so. As you have staked most on and trusted most in Spartans, luck, and hopes, so in all these you will find yourselves most completely deluded.

And so it turned out. All the adult males of Melos were exterminated, and the women and children sold into slavery.

The final point about the war that I think deserves consideration is the gradual brutalizing of sensibilities that accompanied it (and—according to Thucydides—can be expected to accompany *all* protracted wars). Among many instances I select two. The first concerns an episode about which Thucydides does not write, since it takes place in the year 406, about five years after his own history breaks off. In that year the Athenians won their last great sea-battle of the war, at Arginusae. Unfortunately, the victory was marred for the Athenians by the fact that a gale blew up immediately afterwards, with the result that a dozen disabled Athenian ships went down, with enormous loss of life. The eight generals claimed that they had in fact despatched two captains and forty-seven ships to rescue as many survivors from the sea and the disabled ships as possible, and that they could hardly be blamed if a sudden gale had rendered the job impossible. But the Assembly (over-) reacted with what Thucydides would no doubt have

dubbed "typical" brutality and irrationality. In flat contradiction of their own constitutional rules they voted to
condemn to death the six generals present (two had fled,
before they could be arrested), and sentence was carried out
immediately. Only one man on Council stood out to the end
arguing that the vote was unconstitutional: his name was
Socrates.

The second episode is mentioned almost in passing by
Thucydides, and characteristically he offers no comment upon
it, though everything is implied, and it serves in as vivid a
way as I know to show how he felt about the chain-reaction
of savagery that protracted war has a habit of activating. The
year is 413, and the Athenians, unable to use the services of
a number of Thracian mercenaries, instruct them to return
home, under the command of an Athenian officer, Diitrephes.
On their way back, they are told, they would do Athens a
favour if they wreaked a little mayhem on the coastal cities
friendly to Sparta. Let Thucydides finish the story (the 'he'
of the account is Diitrephes):

> He first landed them at Tanagra and carried off some plunder
> in a quick raid; then he sailed across the Euripus in the evening
> from Chalcis in Euboea, landed in Boeotia, and led them
> against Mycalessus. He spent the night unobserved near the
> temple of Hermes, which is nearly two miles from Mycalessus,
> and at daybreak assaulted the city, which is not a big one, and
> captured it. The inhabitants were caught off their guard, since
> they never expected that anyone would come so far from the
> sea to attack them. Their wall, too, was weak and in some
> places had collapsed, while in others it had not been built at
> all high, and the gates were open, since they had no fear of
> being attacked. The Thracians burst into Mycalessus, sacked
> the houses and temples, and butchered the inhabitants, sparing
> neither the young nor the old, but methodically killing every-
> one they met, women and children alike, and even the farm

animals and every living thing they saw. For the Thracian race, like all the most bloodthirsty barbarians, are always particularly bloodthirsty when everything is going their own way. So now there was confusion on all sides and death in every shape and form. Among other things, they broke into a boys' school, the largest in the place, into which the children had just entered, and killed every one of them. Thus disaster fell upon the entire city, a disaster more complete than any, more sudden and more horrible.

I have spent a good deal of time discussing the Peloponnesian War, for two reasons. First, it introduces us to the mind of one of the most thoughtful—not to say disturbing—writers that Athens ever produced, and that is worthwhile in itself; and secondly, it puts us finally in a position to offer some sort of assessment of fifth-century Athenian democracy. We might begin, I think, with a word of caution about two rather misleading sources of information and/or evaluation: I mean the ancient authorities on the one hand and our own twentieth-century political instincts on the other. Athens' major literary sons tended to be from the small educated class, and their background and sympathies were almost invariably aristocratic. One characteristic which seems to be a feature of large numbers of Greek aristocrats was a love of 'order', as against egalitarianism, and it consequently comes as no surprise to find Athens' more significant writers, like Thucydides and Plato, sympathizing more with the disciplined Spartans than with what they considered their own egalitarian but inefficient, reckless, and at times apparently self-destructive compatriots.

Their *prima facie* case is not a silly one. One doesn't have to be an Athenian aristocrat to suspect that Thucydides was absolutely right that the heated atmosphere of the Assembly was the wrong place for formulating war-policy in particular, and many would agree that the lot-system may have been valuable as a barrier to the acquisition of personal power but was absurd as a principle of civic efficiency. The same could be said for the maximum one-year civic appointments and two-year Council appointments; good, perhaps, from the point of view of the general political education of a significant portion of the citizen-body, but hardly conducive to the accumulation of an ongoing body of experience. As for the technique of Ostracism, the Athenians themselves soon came to realize how open to abuse and counter-productive to their interests it could be, and seem to have abandoned it after the Hyperbolus fiasco of 417. As far as the Spartans are concerned, we have already heard Thucydides talking about the moderation and level-headedness of their attitudes, in contrast with the tempestuousness and rashness of the Athenians, and the way the war ended no doubt confirmed him and others in his estimation. When Athens capitulated, several of Sparta's allies demanded that she be treated in exactly the way she had treated Melos; her adult male population should be exterminated, and the women and children enslaved. Instead, Sparta imposed remarkably moderate terms, and Athens as a state survived, though her Empire had gone. One wonders whether she would have treated Sparta so generously, had events gone the other way.

If we leave the ancient authorities for a moment and look at Athenian institutions through twentieth-century eyes, it is no less easy to be critical. But the danger of mis-using hindsight is never absent. In such a situation, the key to understanding seems to me to lie in contextualization. "Given prevailing socio-political institutions," we should ask, "in what way (if any) did fifth-century Athenian institutions represent progress?" On several fronts, we can assume at the outset, little or *no* progress was made; to expect progress in every sphere, as some critics seem to do, seems to me unfair and patronizing. For example, it is frequently pointed out with crushing obviousness that Athenian democracy was built on a slave-base. This is true, and horrible, and cannot afford to be forgotten; but two things should be said. First, there were slaves and slaves, and for what it is worth, Athens' treatment of *its* slave population seems to have been consistently more humane than Sparta's treatment of the Helots; and secondly, till the time of the Industrial Revolution slavery was assumed by *most* of mankind to be an inevitable part of the economic scene.

Others have pointed out how little women appear to have progressed in Athenian society, the few who did so apparently making progress along disreputably sexist lines, like Aspasia, mistress of Pericles. And the point is well taken. While in many ways remarkably forward-looking, Athens was in several other respects pretty much a child of its age, and should be simply recognized as such. But little or nothing is gained, it seems to me, from stressing those areas in Athens' social system in which things stood relatively still; whereas something might just be gained if we concentrate on features which were new. Even in this area there is much that can be criticized, as we have seen, but it must be pointed out that it was an age when democracy was a new and fledgling thing, and errors, blunders, and abuses might have been expected. As an institution involving people at all, Athenian democracy could and did succumb to the corruption engendered by power just as much as other social systems before and after, and in this regard Thucydides' account will always stand as a warning. (We can be sure, for example, that he would have been unsurprised by My Lai.) But in the long run, it seems to me, the germinal ideas themselves have proved more lasting than those who first attempted to implement them could ever have imagined, and it is surely for this reason that we still look back on fifth-century Athenian democracy as a watershed in our political progress. Ostracism may have been an extreme device, but the man who first devised it had his heart in the right place, and we now take it for granted that we can and should, by the use of the vote, turn out governments that prove unacceptable to the majority. The Athenian legal system may have had a lot wrong with it, but the principle of trial by one's peers is one that most people still gratefully accept. It was also Athens who introduced, however imperfectly, the system of payment for public office—a principle we now take for granted, and just as importantly, a Draconian system of accountability *after* one's term of office (!)—a principle we should perhaps start taking a little more seriously. Lastly, and most importantly, it was Athens who—however imperfectly and restrictively in our judgment she defined her *own* citizen-body—pioneered the principle that all who are governed have a right to direct input into *how* they are governed, the force of each and every adult individual in society being the force of a single vote in crucial political decision-making. If in most current democracies that decision-making is largely a matter of the election of representatives, rather than one of direct participation in political and civic life, the general principle remains the same, and credit for its elaboration lies with Athens.

4   The Artistic Achievement

Surely, of all creatures that have life and will, we women
Are the most wretched. When, for an extravagant sum,
We have bought a husband, we must then accept him as
Possessor of our body. This is to aggravate
Wrong with worse wrong. Then the great question: will the
    man
We get be bad or good? For women, divorce is not
Respectable; to repel the man, not possible.

. . . . . .

                    Should he grow tired
Of what he finds at home, he can go out, and find
A cure for tediousness. We wives are forced to look
To one man only. And, they tell us, we at home
Live free from danger, they go out to battle: fools!
I'd rather stand three times in the front line than bear
One child.

That isn't something from Ibsen or Shaw or Beckett; it's
a few lines from the *Medea* of Euripides, first played on the
Athenian stage in March of 431 B.C., when Athens and Sparta
had ceased communicating, and the Great War was imminent.
It's as good an introduction as I know to a feature of fifth-
century Athenian democracy that has gone down in history:
its enormous achievements in the arts, and in particular in the
field of drama. In this she stands alone; over a century earlier
Sparta had simply abandoned the arts as a component of the
civilized life, the better to concentrate her energies on the

production of a no-nonsense 'soldier-state.' In this respect she was an arrested society, and we can safely confine our attention to Athens.

The origins of Athenian tragedy are obscure, but its beginning is traditionally dated to the year 534. It was from the outset an art-form parasitic upon particular religious festivals that the Athenians celebrated, above all the great Spring festival associated with Dionysus, god of vigour and fertility and the joy of life. As part of a given festival it became traditional to dramatize something of the story of the gods and heroes associated with the festival, and within a short time Greek tragedy as we now recognize it was born. Let me just make a few general points about it before offering some detailed illustrations. First of all, given the occasions for which they were composed, Greek tragedies were played in a fairly reverential (though not necessarily reverent!) atmosphere; the nearest modern analogue I can think of would be, say, the performance in the nave of some abbey of Eliot's *Murder in the Cathedral*. I choose that play deliberately, because it illustrates a second point: Greek audiences had a very good idea of the story before they went in to see the play. If, as it happened, both Sophocles and Euripides wrote plays called *Electra*, the interest for the audience lay, not in the re-hearing of a time-honoured tale of matricide but in *how* it was told, and what new insights the dramatist might succeed in conveying. Which brings me to a third point: dramatists were expected in a very serious sense to say things of *importance*. Till they ran into a rival force—the Sophists— in the mid-fifth century, they along with Homer and some of the better-known poets were looked upon as spokesmen for the divine to a people who did not have a Bible as we understand it. So we must expect a certain intensity in Greek drama: thought-provoking things said about perennially thorny moral, social, and theological problems to an audience that expects to come away from the experience with its mind stretched a little.

The high period of Greek tragedy coincides with Athens' rise to power, her cold-war with Sparta, and then the twenty-seven years of the Great War itself. From that period a number of tragic dramas have survived: seven by Aeschylus, seven by Sophocles and nineteen by Euripides. Who their audience consisted of is a matter of some controversy. We know that in the *fourth* century the audience consisted of a wide cross-section of the population, including women, children and slaves. Whether this was equally true earlier on we cannot be sure of, as the evidence is unclear; I'm inclined myself to believe that universal access was the case from very early on, subject to the limitation that adult male citizens were seated first, with the rest admitted afterwards to whatever space was left. The space available, by the way, was large; a huge, open-air amphitheatre accommodating perhaps 12-15,000 people. I used the phrase 'universal access,' and that brings me to my concluding introductory point: the so-called 'festival-fund.' In an earlier talk I mentioned how from the year 462 onwards Athens started to offer nominal *payment* for jury-service, for certain civic posts and even eventually for attendance at the Assembly. As part of this general encouragement to participate in public affairs, they also offered from their festival-fund a small sum to citizens to allow them to attend the theatre—the theatre being viewed by Athens as a major force in the expansion of the social and intellectual sensitivities of its citizens, and in its own way as powerful an educational and mind-expanding arena of experience as those other great arenas, the law-courts and the Assembly.

Let's look now at the tragedians themselves, and explore for a brief while a few examples of their contribution to Athens' civic and cultural life. Aeschylus was born in Athens in 525, and lived the first half of his life in tumultuous times. As a teenager he was there when Athens finally got rid of its tyrants; a few years later he was there when the momentous civic reforms of Cleisthenes were implemented; and as a man of thirty-five actually fought in Athens' victorious army when they defeated the Persians at Marathon. By the time he was in his mid-forties the Persian menace was finally over, and for his last two decades he watched and participated in Athens' attempts to live her new, democratic way of life and cope with the sorts of problems it entailed. In his life-time he had seen violence and conflict, and in some measure their resolution also; the aggression of Persia, for example, had been broken by determined and intelligent resistance, while the social conflicts within Athens itself had been in large measure resolved by the brilliant compromise-legislation of Cleisthenes. He had good grounds for optimism and pride in his city's achievements, and this is I think reflected in his art. Let's look for a moment at one example, the *Oresteia*, which many consider his greatest achievement. In the three dramas united under that name he re-tells, in spell-binding poetry and a tone of unmatched moral fervour, a tale very familiar to his audience. Long ago, two brothers, vying for succession to the throne of Argos, had by their actions triggered off a sequence of bloody vendettas that by *accepted* law seemed to be endless. Thyestes had first seduced his brother Atreus' wife, and Atreus revenged himself by murdering two of Thyestes' sons and serving them up to him at a banquet. An unjust act had bred an unjuster one, and a curse now settled on the descendants of Atreus. He had two sons, Agamemnon and Menelaus, who eventually married two sisters, Clytemnestra and Helen. After some time Helen eloped to Troy with one of the princes of that city, Paris, and Agamemnon joined forces with his brother to put together a huge force of Greeks to sail to Troy and get her back. At this point the curse on the family manifests itself: Agamemnon is driven by–what? God? Necessity? Circumstance? that of course is the heart of the problem–to perform an act which by accepted law automatically guarantees that the curse will carry over into the *next* generation, and which as a by-product blinds *him* into *further* misdeeds in the future that will by some inexorable law of revenge seal his own fate even more securely. He is at Aulis, waiting with his fleet to set sail, but the wind changes. The fleet is becalmed for months, and he is eventually persuaded by a seer that the only way he will ever get to Troy is by the human sacrifice of his daughter Iphigeneia. He tricks his wife into sending the girl to Aulis, where she is put to death, and the fleet sails to Troy. After a ten-year siege, Troy falls, and Agamemnon returns home in triumph, with a captive Trojan princess, Cassandra, unwillingly at his side and the memory of a pillaged and desecrated Troy behind him. While he has been away, however, the Avenging Furies have been arranging a little reception for him. Thyestes' *surviving* son Aegistheus had become the lover of Clytemnestra, and with his help she murders Agamemnon as soon as he returns home, on the reasonable-looking grounds that *he* had–among other infamies–murdered their daughter ten years earlier. But this murder in turn brings out the curse in the family once more; being murder, it too by accepted law must be avenged. The scene switches to a final generation. The son of Agamemnon and Clytemnestra, Orestes, avenges his father's murder by murdering her and her lover, and is driven to a state of madness by the Avenging Furies, who among other things see it as their duty to avenge all crimes of matricide; they are not deterred by the fact that Apollo, acting for Zeus, the Supreme God himself, had actually *commanded* Orestes to kill his mother!

Why is Aeschylus re-telling this bizarre and bloody story? Like most great dramatists, he doesn't tell us in clear and straightforward terms; and critics have argued over the matter ever since. In spite of this, I think one or two basic points can be made with relative safety. The question, What is Justice, will always be of interest to right-thinking people, and we can be sure Aeschylus was aware of the particular importance of the problem to his compatriots. Athens was now a democracy, and in a democracy enormous numbers of people who had previously been *excluded* from civic life and the process of the implementation of law were now fully *involved* in such things and all the dilemmas and painful decisions that they bring in their train. Collective responsibility now lay with the *people*; and they looked to dramatists like Aeschylus— among others—for some sort of moral guidance in such matters. Whether Aeschylus felt he could offer such guidance we don't know; but his resolution to the Orestes story suggests to me that he may have felt he could. In the final play of his trilogy, we see the Avenging Furies and Apollo brought to court—a court presided over by Athens' own patroness, the Goddess Athena. The Furies stress the ancient law that matricides be punished; hence Orestes' present punishment. Apollo stresses that Orestes' deed was itself the revenge for a father's murder and divinely sanctioned at that. So Orestes was *unfairly* punished. The jury consists of a venerable Athenian institution, the Areopagus, a body of citizens all of whom had served their city as senior magistrates. They are understandably torn by the dilemma and their vote is a tie. Athena casts the tie-breaking vote, and it is a vote for reason, compassion, and the New Order.

The *Oresteia* was produced in the year 458, four years after the reformer Ephialtes had stripped the venerable Areopagus of most of its powers, leaving it with little except power to judge cases of homicide. For purposes of Aeschylus' play, however, that was enough. The Areopagus, guided by Athena, clearly represents for him the triumph of *reasoned judgment* in matters of homicide over blind and ineluctable laws of vendetta. In a less civilized age, when no *legal* redress of any sophisticated sort was at hand, murder tended to be avenged by a relative of the murdered person, and the principle became enshrined in the public consciousness as some sort of Natural Law. In a more civilized age, represented by the Athens of his day, Aeschylus seems to be saying, such a supposed law is seen to be barbarous, and has been rightly superseded by a better state of affairs, which we might dub 'Due Process of Law.' The new law has *something* of the old in it, in that it is still rightly an object of fear to the transgressor, like the old law of irrational, knee-jerk vendetta; but it now combines compassion with justice, and esteems moderation and reasoned argument more highly than violence and irrationality. It is not, I think, too much to say that for Aeschylus such attitudes are the crowning achievement of Athens' democratic system and a guiding principle for her continued moral health as a society.

As a brief illustration of his dramatic art I have chosen two short items from the *Agamemnon*, the first play in his trilogy. First, a portion of an ode chanted by the Chorus, which consists of fifteen old men of Argos, the city from which Helen eloped to Troy. They talk of the pain of loss felt by Menelaus as he dreams of her, and the anger and resentment of the *people* of Argos, as they see their fathers, sons and husbands die on the plains of Troy—for whom? For an adulteress.

> Lightly she crossed the threshold
> And left her palace, fearless
> Of what should wake her fears;
> And took to Troy as dowry
> Destruction, blood, and tears.
> There lies her husband fasting,
> Dumb in his stricken room.

. . . . . .

Visions of her beset him
With false and fleeting pleasure
When dreams are dark and deep.
He sees her, runs to hold her;
And, through his fingers slipping,
Lightly departs his treasure,
The dream he cannot keep,
Wafted on wings that follow
The shadowy paths of sleep.

Such are the searching sorrows
This royal palace knows,
While through the streets of Argos
Grief yet more grievous grows,
With all our manhood gathered
So far from earth of Hellas;
As in each home unfathered,
Each widowed bed, the whetted
Sword of despair assails
Hearts where all hope has withered
And angry hate prevails.
They sent forth men to battle,
But no such men return;
And home, to claim their welcome,
Come ashes in an urn.

For War's a banker, flesh his gold.
There by the furnace of Troy's field,
Where thrust meets thrust, he sits to hold
His scale, and watch the spear-point sway;
And back to waiting homes he sends
Slag from the ore, a little dust
To drain hot tears from hearts of friends;
Good measure, safely stored and sealed
In a convenient jar—the just
Price for the man they sent away.

They praise him through their tears, and say,
'He was a soldier!' or, 'He died
Nobly, with death on every side!'
And fierce resentment mutters low,
'Yes—for another's wife!'

And now the first words of Clytemnestra, after the murder
of Agamemnon. The palace gates open to reveal her standing
over the body, which is lying in a silver bath and enveloped
in a large purple robe. By him lies Cassandra.

I said, not long since, many things to match the time;
All which, that time past, without shame I here unsay.
How else, when one prepares death for an enemy
Who seems a friend—how else net round the deadly trap
High enough to forestall the victim's highest leap?
A great while I have pondered on this trial of strength.
At long last the pitched battle came, and victory:
Here where I struck I stand and see my task achieved.
Yes, this is my work, and I claim it. To prevent
Flight or resistance foiling death, I cast on him,
As one who catches fish, a vast voluminous net,
That walled him round with endless wealth of woven folds;
And then I struck him, twice. Twice he cried out and groaned;
And then fell limp. And as he lay I gave a third
And final blow, my thanks for prayers fulfilled, to Zeus,
Lord of the lower region, Saviour—of dead men!
So falling he belched forth his life; with cough and retch
There spurted from him bloody foam in a fierce jet,
And spreading, spattered me with drops of crimson rain;
While I exulted as the sown cornfield exults
Drenched with the dew of heaven when buds burst forth in
Spring.

So stands the case, Elders of Argos. You may be,
As you choose, glad or sorry; I am jubilant.

The *Oresteia*, like most of Greek tragedy, is about conflict and its resolution, and limits of time have confined me to talking about only one aspect of it. But we have just heard Clytemnestra, and that brings me to a *sub*-conflict in the drama that will continue to be of importance throughout the history of Greek tragedy. That is, the conflict in the heart of a strong woman when her emotions, or ambitions, or sheer sense of justice, run into the road-block of restrictions and role-patterns imposed upon her by a male-dominated society. We have already heard Medea speak; the tradition of such frustrated complaints, and the uncontained violence and destruction to which they are so often the prelude, goes straight back to Clytemnestra.

The second of Athens' great tragedians was Sophocles. Born in 496, he lived for ninety years, that is to within two years of the end of the Peloponnesian War. Unlike Aeschylus, for whom God is ultimately just and all will be well, if we can but learn from suffering, Sophocles lived through a period in Athens' history when events were leading many to doubt whether so optimistic a vision of things was really appropriate. At the end of the *Oresteia* we leave (or are meant to leave) reinforced in our basic optimism, in spite of the problem of suffering; at the end of Sophocles' *Antigone* things are a little less straightforward. Sophocles is still clearly in the Aeschylean tradition in his basic belief that divine laws cannot be flouted without punishment, but it is nonetheless Antigone, the innocent upholder of those laws, who actually dies, not King Creon. He is punished, of course, and will, like Aeschylean man, learn through suffering. What was his crime? A combination of arrogance and extremism; 'playing God,' if you like. This sounds like Agamemnon; but time and circumstance add an interesting twist to the situation. The year the play was produced was 442. Athens was at the height of her imperialist phase, and was, in many ways, as we have seen, already starting to become corrupted by the power that she had accumulated.

At Athens' helm was the nearest thing she had to a king—Pericles. Was Sophocles' great play a cry of alarm? A call to return to the finer civic virtues of a generation earlier, when the justice dispensed by the Areopagus *coincided with*, rather than contradicted, divine justice? No one can be certain, but it seems to me a reasonable guess. We do know that Pericles was looked upon as unjust and as a despot by many of the subject-allies, and pilloried as a tyrant by some of the comic poets of the day. Perhaps Sophocles shared their alarm, and was here suggesting to an uneasy audience that Athens' accumulation of power had been matched by a disturbing tendency to overstep the mark in the moral scheme of things and to play God—a tendency instantiated with particular clarity in the activities of her First Citizen? In the most famous Ode in the *Antigone* the Chorus talks of civilized man's achievements, and also of his reckless tendency to go to extremes and transgress Laws far more fundamental than laws *he* ever instituted. It may remind you of *Thucydides'* views on Athens' peculiar (and dangerous) tendency to reckless and extreme decisions, like for example the decision to destroy Mitylene.

> The world is full of wonders, but
> There's nothing in this world more wonderful than Man.
> This creature dares to cross the sea
> When winter gales reduce it to a foaming froth,
> And still continues though the roaring waves tower round
>   him.
> Earth, that oldest of the gods, he tames,
> Undying though she is, and tireless.
> Year in, year out, his plough goes up and down
> The furrows, and his horses strain to turn the soil.
>
> The same Man fabricates devices to ensnare
> The guileless birds and savage animals,
> And fashions close-meshed nets to reap the harvest

Of the sea; he has a plan for everything.
By means of his contraptions he is master
Of the beasts that roam the mountain-slopes,
And now has taught the rough-maned horse
And tireless mountain-bull to bear the yoke.

And he has taught himself the art of speech,
And elevated thought and social sensibility,
And how, when living out of doors,
To keep away from frost and stinging rain.
There is no end to his inventiveness;
No future challenge makes him doubt his power to cope.
Diseases hitherto untamed he now controls;
Yet how to get away from Death eludes his cleverness.

He has within his power a skill
And subtlety beyond all expectation.
This he uses sometimes well, sometimes despicably,
As when he flouts his country's laws
Or breaks an oath sworn by his gods.
He builds high cities. But better cityless, I think,
The man whose life is arrogant and reckless.
Such a man can stay away from me;
He'll never share my hearth and company.

If I am not over-estimating the implications of this play,
Sophocles was, at the time he wrote it, no less convinced of
the inevitable working out of divine justice than was his great
predecessor Aeschylus, but considerably *less* optimistic about
the moral health of Athens itself. Pessimism on *both* fronts
seems to me a hall-mark of his younger contemporary,
Euripides. I say 'seems,' because a peculiar feature of Euripides
is his ambiguity. For him, as for his predecessors, drama lies
in the honest confrontation of contradiction, but his solutions
are seldom clear, and never simple. That no doubt accounts
for the fact that over the years he has been called a misogynist,
a feminist, a pacifist, a jingoist, a sceptic, a free-thinker, an

idealist, and a lot more. The variety, and at times mutual exclusiveness of the list suggests that the whole approach might be wrong. More plausible, it seems to me, is the view that as a dramatist he is committed to the *examination* of *contradiction*, rather than to any particular solutions. Indeed, as a student of the New Learning, he may well have believed that no clear solutions were possible. The New Learning is something I wish to discuss in the final lecture. Suffice it to say for the moment that from about the mid-fifth century onwards itinerant teachers called Sophists came to exercise a greater and greater influence on the minds of Athenians. One of them, Protagoras, seems to have had a particular influence on Euripides, not least with his doctrine that whatever the problem you pose yourself, there will always be both a case and a counter-case for whatever solution is proposed. So if Euripides saw it as his job to *teach* the Athenians *anything* at all, it was presumably a *technique* he would have wanted to teach them – the technique of examination of both sides of the question. Thanks to this technique, the greatness of so many of his plays lies in the expanded consciousness they invariably generate of the subtlety and complexity of critical social and moral issues. From among many such issues I shall confine my attention to three that exercised his attention for a lifetime: the consequences of war, the sufferings of women (and what such sufferings can lead to), and the place of reason and emotion in the balanced personality.

Euripides' first play was produced in 455, three years after Aeschylus' *Oresteia*, and for the next thirty years or so further plays teemed from his brain. A large number of these dealt with women – not of course overtly contemporary women, but in the accepted tradition of tragedy women from the mytho- logical past. They can be summed up roughly as plays about 'bad' women (like Medea, who murders her children) and 'suffering' women (like Phaedra, who commits suicide over

95

unrequited love). The violence of some of the female villains led many observers in antiquity to dub Euripides a misogynist; the heart-rending sufferings of other women portrayed in his plays have led a number of more recent critics to dub him a feminist and crusading social reformer. Both descriptions seem to me doubtful. What Euripides surely *was* convinced of is that villains of either sex are made, not born such, and the extant plays are in large part a subtle investigation of what sort of situation, and what sort of treatment, could have *produced* such violence. The *Medea* seems to me a good example. Like Clytemnestra in the *Agamemnon*, Medea turns to murder out of frustration at the fact that in a man's universe her husband has exercised what he takes to be his prerogative: in this case to divorce her for a younger woman. If Euripides was a misogynist, it is hard to guess it from the first part of this play, in which Medea constructs a powerful indictment of the injustice of her situation – and by implication, of the situation of most Greek women of Euripides' own time. With rare exceptions, a woman's lot in fifth-century Athens was to marry (or rather: 'get married': her marriage was arranged by the fathers of bride and bridegroom), bear and bring up children, and manage a household. She did not participate in civic life, except for attendance at some of the religious festivals, trips to the market, and so on. By no stretch of the imagination could the equality-among-males that was at least partly true of Athenian citizens be said to apply to the average man-and-wife situation. There are only two exceptions to this rule: the first is found amongst the daughters of rich and powerful (and better educated) families. We find Alcibiades' wife, for example, divorcing *him* because of his continual association with *hetaerae*; penniless wives, by contrast (that is, the majority), to whom marriage, for all its problems, seemed to be their biggest single protection, were understandably unprepared to face the hazardous future that such a move might involve. I mentioned *hetaerae*, and that brings me to the second exception: that varied group of women, usually slaves or resident aliens, who made a living as professional entertainers and companions to the rich. They were frequently musicians, and one of their many roles was to perform at the women's religious festivals; another, better-known one was to provide music and sex at male drinking parties. The poorest among them lived in and worked from the brothels near the waterfront; the richest lived lives not unlike those of what Webster has called "the *grandes cocottes*" of Edwardian Paris. Aspasia, for example, mistress of Pericles, was a *hetaera* from Miletus; she was clearly a woman of sophistication, and one in no way strait-jacketed by prevailing social mores. As such, she was no doubt a combined threat and object of contempt to the sober majority in society–male *and* female–and it comes as no surprise to find her the constant butt of jokes by contemporary comic dramatists.

Whatever the *average* Athenian felt about the whole question of the role and status of women in a man's world, Euripides the dramatist clearly saw it as one of the many forms of tension of which great drama is made. Operating by the proxy of mythology, as always, he exposes the situation in play after play to the harsh glare of dialectical investigation, and we can be sure that time and again he sent home thinking members of his audience feeling profoundly uncomfortable about social attitudes that most of them had hitherto accepted as self-evidently good and reasonable.

The same sort of dramatic tension he seems to have found in the clash between reason and emotion. Here his own views are a little easier to discern, and he turns out to be a spokesman for the virtue of moderation in both areas, suggesting that particular forms of tragic outcome stem from failure to achieve this. While Medea's *situation*, for example, serves as an *extenu-*

ation of the crime of murder, Euripides intimates (as a debating-point, if nothing else) that her own lack of self-control, particularly in the matter of sexual jealousy, is a major factor in the crime, and something for which blame is to be laid at least partially at her own door. In the *Hippolytus*, likewise, the two main characters come to a grievous end for similar reasons. Phaedra, tormented with sexual longing for her stepson Hippolytus, kills herself when told that Hippolytus has come to know of it; Hippolytus the misogynist, conceding nothing whatsoever to sexual desire and priding himself on his chastity, is at the opposite end of the emotional spectrum to Phaedra, but just as doomed to a tragic end. There is a middle way, Euripides seems to be suggesting, some twilight world in which reason and emotion meet on moderate and mutually respectful terms; and that is the world of sanity and goodness. As it is, we only have to listen to a few lines from Hippolytus to realise that anyone so immoderate and uncontrolled (he has just learned of Phaedra's passion for him) is marked for destruction—

> Women! This coin which men find counterfeit!
> Why, why, Lord Zeus, did you put them in the world,
> in the light of the sun? If you were so determined
> to breed the race of man, the source of it
> should not have been women. Men might have dedicated
> in your own temples images of gold,
> silver, or weight of bronze, and thus have bought
> the seed of progeny,. . .each being given
> his worth in sons according to the assessment
> of his gift's value. So we might have lived
> in houses free of the taint of women's presence.
> But now, to bring this plague into our homes
> we drain the fortunes of our homes.
>
> . . . . . .
>
> For the father who begets her, rears her up,

must add a dowry gift to pack her off
to another's house and thus be rid of the load.
And he again that takes the cursed creature
rejoices and enriches his heart's jewel
with expensive adornment, beauty heaped on vileness.
With lovely clothes the poor wretch tricks her out,
spending the wealth that underprops his house.
That husband has the easiest life whose wife
is a mere nothingness, a simple fool,
uselessly sitting by the fireside.
I hate a clever woman–God forbid
that I should ever have a wife at home
with more than woman's wits! Lust breeds mischief
in the clever ones. The limits of their minds
deny the stupid lecherous delights.

Finally, there is the ever-present phenomenon of *war*. When the Great War begins, Euripides responds with a series of plays containing sentiments to swell all patriotic hearts. But typically, he finds tragic tension even here. In the *Suppliant Women*, for example, we have a situation in which a group of seven women from Argos, whose sons have been killed in battle against Thebes, come to Athens with the request that King Theseus help them recover the bodies of their sons, whom the Thebans, contrary to all sacred custom, have flung out unburied for the dogs to eat. Theseus finally agrees, uttering sentiments about his city to flatter the ego of all patriotic Athenians. But the second half of the play is ashes in the mouth, as the bodies are brought on stage, and we hear the heart-rending lamentations of the mothers. What started off as basically a play in praise of Athens as a civilizing influence turns into a description of the inhumanity of war–and in particular its inhumanity in the sufferings it inflicts on non-combatants, especially women. As the Great War dragged on, Euripides, like Thucydides, clearly found less and less to be patriotic about, and his distress reached its culmination in 415, to judge by the final play of a trilogy he produced in that year—*Trojan Woman*. In the previous winter, it will be remembered, the Athenians had put to death all men on the island of Melos, and enslaved the women and children. When this happened, something must have finally broken in Euripides, and in a state of controlled frenzy he went back to the story of the Trojan War as his prototype for the inhumanity of war. The great siege is over; the Greeks are finally victorious—and proceed at once to treat the vanquished with the immoderation and recklessness that will in the end inevitably bring retribution on their own heads. Meanwhile, the innocent suffer. The royal women of Troy, having seen their men wiped out in war or exterminated after it, have been allotted as booty to the various Greek generals, and the play deals with the short period between the time of that allotment and their departure into slavery and enforced concubinage. Hecuba, mother of the Trojan hero Hector, has lived to see all her sons killed in war, her husband murdered, and now all her daughters and herself enslaved—all except one daughter Polyxena, who like Iphigeneia, daughter of Agamemnon, is slaughtered as a peace-offering to the gods by the Greeks, in hopes of a safe return home. But the victors are not through yet. In a final act of savagery they decree that Hector's little child Astyanax—who might after all grow up one day and live to avenge his father!—be thrown from the city walls. Nothing that I can say can catch the powerful impact of this play; I can only remark that I have never yet met a person who has seen it performed who does not consider it one of the greatest statements ever penned on the brutalizing effects of protracted war. If Thucydides' Melian dialogue was the bare bones of such a statement, here is its flesh and blood. Of its many memorable passages I select what seems to me the most powerful. The shattered body of the boy Astyanax has been brought onto the stage on a shield, and laid down quietly

before the audience's eyes. His grandmother Hecuba looks at
the child, gazes around her, and speaks.

Achaeans! All your strength is in your spears, not in
the mind. What were you afraid of, that it made you kill
this child so savagely? That Troy, which fell, might be
raised from the ground once more? Your strength meant
    nothing, then.
When Hector's spear was fortunate, and numberless
strong hands were there to help him, we were still destroyed.
Now when the city is fallen and the Phrygians slain,
this baby terrified you? I despise the fear
which is pure terror in a mind unreasoning.

O darling child, how wretched was this death. You might
have fallen fighting for your city, grown to man's
age, and married, and with the king's power like a god's,
and died happy, if there is any happiness here.
But no. You grew to where you could see and learn, my child,
yet your mind was not old enough to win advantage
of fortune. How wickedly, poor boy, your fathers' walls,
Apollo's handiwork, have crushed your pitiful head
tended and trimmed to ringlets by your mother's hand,
and the face she kissed once, where the brightness now is blood
shining through the torn bones—too horrible to say more.
O little hands, sweet likenesses of Hector's once,
now you lie broken at the wrists before my feet;
and mouth beloved whose words were once so confident,
you are dead; and all was false, when you would lean across
my bed, and say: "Mother, when you die I will cut
my long hair in your memory, and at your grave
bring companies of boys my age, to sing farewell."
It did not happen; now I, a homeless, childless, old
woman must bury your poor corpse, which is so young.
Alas for all the tendernesses, my nursing care,
and all your slumbers gone. What shall the poet say,
what words will he inscribe upon your monument?
*Here lies a little child the Argives killed, because
they were afraid of him.*

It is Euripides' final statement on war to his compatriots. His later plays exist in a state of suspended animation, part fantasy, part romance, part escapism. The great spirit of passionate enquiry has apparently been beaten to its knees, and all he has for comfort is his art. Here is an ode on Old Age from the *Heracles*, written some time about this date, when Euripides himself was no doubt feeling the advancing years:

Youth I've always loved.
Old age is horrible!. . .it weighs more heavily
Upon my head than all of
Aetna's rocks, and shrouds my eyes
In light of darkness.
I don't want the riches
Of some Asiatic despot!
Houses stuffed with gold
Are no exchange for vigorous youth—
A man's most radiant possession,
Be times prosperous or poor.
I loathe lugubrious old age,
That deals in death! If only
It would sink beneath the sea,
Or put on wings and fly away!
Why ever did it show its face
In human homes and cities?

If gods had minds
(And men intelligence)
They'd mark the virtuous for all to see
By granting them two periods
Of vibrant manhood; after death such persons
Would return to earth and sunlight
And complete a second course,
While meanness would have just a single span.
And then one could distinguish
Good and evil men,
The way a host of stars is glimpsed

By sailors through the clouds.
But, as it is, the gods
Have granted man no clear conception
Of what vice and virtue are;
What grows with turning Time
Is just our store of wealth. . . .

Yet I shall not cease linking hand in hand
The goddesses of Beauty and of Inspiration—
For no union gives greater joy.
I'd rather die than live deprived of Art!
If only I could always be among the victors!
But old poets can invoke
The goddess Memory.
I still can sing the victory-song
Of Heracles, in company with
Bromios, who gives us wine,
And plays his seven-stringed lyre
And Libyan flute.
I'll never fail in my devotion to
The goddesses of Inspiration; for they taught me Art.

But the time was not yet. Disillusioned, he left Athens forever in 408, at the age of seventy-six, and retired to Macedon. There one might have expected him to fade quietly away. But the move from the city to the wild mountainous atmosphere did something to his spirits, and the great eagle summoned its strength, stretched its wings, and soared into the sky one final time. The *Bacchae* was staged posthumously in Athens, probably in the year 405, and is thought by many to be his greatest masterpiece. In it he returns to a theme that had always haunted him: the place of reason and emotion in the balanced life. With a last outpouring of wild and tumultuous verbal energy appropriate to the theme he puts the case once more for the importance—and also the danger—of conceding something to the emotional, or Bacchic element within us, and a typically disturbing case it is. But I'd prefer to leave him on a slightly different note. A few years before his death he had written a romantic play called *Iphigeneia among the Taurians*. In this he imagines that Iphigeneia was *not* sacrificed by her father Agamemnon, but was spirited away to safety in Scythia. She eventually returns home, leaving behind the slave-woman who had saved her. In a great Choral Ode the slave-woman speaks of her longing for Greece, and particularly Athens, of her sufferings, and of her despair before the memory of a childhood spent in freedom. The mood, the magnificent language, and the structure of the ode, from sombre beginning to heights of intensity to the quiet, nostalgic coda, constitute for me at any rate one of the purest examples of Euripides' art:

> Blue-bird, plaintively lamenting
> As you skim the crests
> Of rocky head-lands; blue-bird,
> Calling endlessly in song upon your husband
> (Cries replete with meaning for the man who
> understands);
> I, too, a wingless bird,
> Have sorrows matching yours.
> I long for gatherings of Greeks in city-squares;
> I long for Artemis, the guardian of motherhood,
> Whose home is by Mount Cynthus,
> Where the date-palm, delicate to touch,
> And the luxuriant laurel
> And the soft-green olive's sacred bough,
> The child of Leto's birth-pangs, grow;
> And where a swan, upon a lake that swirls
> Its waters round in circling pools,
> Pays honour to the Muses with its clear-voiced
> song.
>
> The tears that fell in streams
> And drowned my cheeks

The day that I was brought from ruined walls
And forced at spear-point
To the enemy's ships, and they set sail!
A piece of merchandize, exchanged for gold,
I travelled to a foreign land,
Where I am now the slave
Of Agamemnon's daughter, priestess
To the goddess Artemis, whose altars here
Are not for sacrifice of sheep. . . .
I envy him whose fate entails
Uninterrupted misery. One never struggles,
                         then,
Against Necessity, for one was reared with
                         it.
Pure misery is something we can bear.
What breaks a man is being brought
To grief when happy times preceded.

You, queen, are going home;
An Argive ship, with fifty oars, will take
                         you.
Mountain Pan himself will guide the blades,
The rhythmic beat provided by
His whistling pipe of reeds.
The prophet-god Apollo will make music
On his seven-stringed lyre
And guide you to that radiant country
Where Athenians have their home.
And I'll be left behind,
While you are borne away by churning oars.
The sails will catch the wind,
And spread across the bows and prow;
And then your ship will surge along its way.

If only I could ride the path
Where those bright horses draw the fiery
                         sun!
If only I were home,

And I could fold
These restless wings upon my back!
If I could join in stately marriage-dances
Once again, as in my girlhood,
When I'd leave my mother's side
And whirl light-heartedly around
The dance-floor with my friends,
Determined to appear the prettiest,
And rouse their envy for my soft, rich hair!
You could not see my face
For lovely veils and clustering curls. . . .

Up to now I have been discussing merely Greek tragedy, and it would be misleading if I left the impression that it did not have a foil. It did; and that was what came to be known as Old Comedy. Of the comic playwrights of the day only one is represented by a number of surviving plays, and that is Aristophanes. His plays are barbed and brilliant, though a little troublesome for the non-specialist, since a fair number of the jokes turn on local situations and events and the part played in them by local worthies—like Cleon. But a bit of background-work is worth the effort. What soon emerges is a mind of wit and sophistication that sees possibilities for comic humour everywhere; it also knows how to appeal to the prejudices of special-interest groups—and not least those who put up the money for the production of his plays! The *Acharnians*, produced in 425, is about a private peace treaty between an Athenian farmer, Dicaeopolis, and the Spartans. One can be sure it went down very well with the hundreds of country-folk who came in for the Festival, in that for the past half-decade they had seen their crops and lands systematically destroyed by the Spartans. The *Knights* was produced a year later, and ridiculed the demagogue Cleon, of whom I have talked before. The *Clouds*, produced in 423, poked fun at the philosopher Socrates, and no doubt appealed to large numbers who at this stage of the war were still prepared merely to *laugh* at Egg-heads; by its end, as Socrates found out, they would be in the mood for uglier ways of expressing their dislike. The *Wasps*, produced in 422, tore into the jury-system, with its easy opportunities for the corruption and bribery of jurymen by the rich and influential.

It's all very funny, in its own scabrous and fecal way, but one soon comes to realize that its author, like Thucydides and Euripides, is haunted—by the War. We saw a hint of this in the theme of the *Acharnians* in 425; it flowered in 421, when he produced a play called *Peace* to commemorate the pending (and ultimately abortive) peace treaty between the two great powers. By 414, one year after the Melos episode, Aristophanes, like Euripides, is apparently in an altered state of consciousness; his play of that year, *The Birds*, deals with two Athenians who leave the city in search of another and better city elsewhere, and for advice in the matter look to—well, Birds. But if *he* is in a state of near-despair, his comic genius has certainly not atrophied, as both the *Birds* shows (it's one of his cleverest plays) and the next play, *Lysistrata*, produced in 411. In this, perhaps the most widely known of his plays, he imagines an Athenian woman, Lysistrata, plotting with a gang of wives of soldiers from other belligerent cities to stage a sex-strike till the men have the intelligence to end the war. It is a theme to which he will return when the war is over; in 392, in his play *Women in Assembly*, he goes the whole way, and writes a play round the notion that men have made such a mess of things that political power should be transferred to women.

Aristophanes, like the tragedians, is clearly worth a lecture to himself, but enough has been said, I think, to suggest that in comic as well as tragic art fifth-century Athens achieved a remarkable level of greatness. We saw in the last lecture how for the citizen-body participation in the political process was a major part of their *raison d'être*: in Pericles' words: "We do not say that a man who takes no interest in politics is a man who minds his own business; we say that he has no business here at all!" Participation in the great *dramatic festivals* was the other side of this same coin, and the *completion* of one's education in citizenship. In a day and age when mass education as we understand it did not exist, these were the two outstanding opportunities that Athens offered its citizens both to contribute to the life and health of the community and to benefit from it, and history has rightly praised it as one of her outstanding achievements. The quality of much of the drama they produced speaks for itself, and the freedom of the atmosphere in *which* it was produced is almost as impressive. If in these past two lectures I have indicated (following Thucydides) some of the *dangers* of such freedom, particularly under war conditions, I cannot in fairness leave the question without ultimately paying my own mite of tribute to the greatness and importance of such freedom as a social, political, and artistic achievement. It may have been equalled, but it has never been surpassed, and Athens will always be acknowledged as its flawed but brilliant pioneering exemplar.

5 The Thinkers

People believe that the gods are begotten, and that they wear clothing like our own, and have a voice and a body.

The Ethiopians make their gods snub-nosed and black; the Thracians make theirs blue-eyed and red-haired.

If oxen and horses and lions had hands, and could draw with their hands and do what man can do, horses would draw the gods in the shape of horses, and oxen in the shape of oxen, each giving the gods bodies similar to their own.

The particular argument-form exemplified in the above quotations is commonly called a *reductio ad absurdum*, and the book from which the words come was written by the Greek thinker Xenophanes of Colophon in the sixth century B.C. He is one of a number of enquiring minds from that early period in Greece's history who pioneered Western philosophy. What distinguishes them from earlier writers is the sort of question they were asking, and the reason why they were asking such questions. Hitherto people had in general agreed (whatever the disagreement over details) that God or the gods made and ruled the world, and that their will dictated human conduct. Questions about man and the world were ultimately answerable, it was felt, in terms of those gods: in the case of the world the gods of the elements, like Hephaestus, god of Fire and Poseidon, god of Water; in the case of man the gods of reason and the various emotions, like Aphrodite, goddess of love, Ares, god of war, Apollo, god of reason, and the greatest of the gods Zeus, god of the great sky and the ultimate justice of things. But by the sixth century momentous changes were taking place in *this* area too, as in those of political theory and practice. A number of thinkers were starting to ask what could be known about the world simply in terms of the world; what could be known about man simply in terms of man; and what—if and when *those* questions have been satisfactorily answered—the role and status (if any) of the traditional gods of Olympus might be? It was the beginning of what we might call a 'scientific' approach to the real—and its effects are still felt by all of us.

By the mid-fifth century the new rationalism was apparent to many thinking people. Just how different it was from older ways of thinking will become clear from a few examples. Here first is the poet Hesiod's account of the origin of the Universe (composed in the eighth century B.C.):

First of all was Chaos born. . . .
From Chaos there sprang Erebos
and dark-robed Night.
From Night the Upper Air was born
and Day, borne in her womb,
the offspring of her love for Erebos.
The Earth's first offspring,
equal to herself, was Heaven
filled with stars, to cover her entire
and be a sure, eternal dwelling-place
for the blessed gods.

And now an account of the world's origins by Anaxagoras, writing about the middle of the fifth century:

Mind controlled the whole world's rotation. . . .At first it began to rotate from a small beginning, but now it rotates over a larger area, and it will rotate over a still larger area. And mind knows all the things that are mingled and separated out and distinguished. . . .And what sort of things were to be, and what sort of things were (but now no longer are), and what now is, and what sort of things will be—all these *mind* arranged, and the rotation in which the stars now rotate and the sun and the moon and the air and the ether. . . .

The gods, you will notice, have gone; what remains is Mind or Intelligence, ordering matter which is simply that—matter. Fire is not some manifestation of Hephaestus, and water is not some manifestation of Poseidon; they are both now simply physical stuff. The 'matter' in question Anaxagoras believed was infinitely divisible; his younger contemporaries Leucippus and Democritus disagreed, and argued that the world consisted (and had *always* consisted) of empty space and chance conglomerations of basic bits of matter that were not further divisible called 'atoms' (a Greek word *meaning* 'things not further divisible'). The world and its operations are accountable for *entirely* in terms of empty space, matter, and what *they* call 'Necessity' and we would nowadays perhaps call the Laws of Motion and Impact. You will notice that even the Mind or Intelligence of which Anaxagoras spoke has now been dispensed with as an explanatory feature of the way things are.

Startling views of the world such as this (which remain startling—and alarming—to millions even now) were not lost on the Sophists, who at about this time were starting to exercise a greater and greater influence on thinking Athenians. The Sophists were itinerant teachers, who sold their educational services to those who could afford them—which in practice meant the fairly affluent families of the day. Their rise to prominence at this time was no accident. In the new democratic Athens the gift of the gab was at a premium; without it, how could one make one's mark in the Assembly, or defend oneself in the Law Courts? Such ability the Sophists professed to be able to teach, and with it they tended to inculcate a basic scepticism which all seemed to share in varying degrees, and which as I have indicated was in the air at the time: scepticism about the world, about the gods, about value-systems, about just about everything which most Greeks had hitherto accepted. To the younger generation, who sat at the feet of these men, it must have been all very liberating and exhilarating; to the older generation, with rare exceptions, it must have been alarming. Imagine the impact, for example, on a good god-fearing Greek of the following statement of the sophist Protagoras:

> Man is the measure of all things: of existing things, that they exist; of nonexistent things, that they do not exist.

Or the following?

> Concerning the gods, I do not know whether they exist or not. For many are the obstacles to knowledge: the obscurity of the subject and the brevity of human life.

Or what would he have thought, on learning from his son, who had just returned from a lecture by the sophist Gorgias, that the thesis for discussion that day had been as follows:

a) Nothing at all exists;
b) Even if it *did* exist, we could have no knowledge of it;
and c) Even if we *did* have knowledge of it, we couldn't *communicate* our knowledge to anyone else.

'Too clever by half' we can be sure was the father's response; or, more likely, something unprintable.

Among these public teachers of the day was Socrates. In the eyes of the general public he was just another Sophist, instilling scepticism of everything sacred into large numbers of young men, who would grow up to become highly influential figures in Athens' political fortunes. As such he was the butt of the comic dramatists of the day, and good for a laugh (if perhaps a somewhat uneasy laugh); as I mentioned earlier, a version of his supposed 'views' (and a marvellously garbled and pompous and comically exaggerated version it is) was shot through with cheerful arrows by Aristophanes in his *Clouds*. And even two generations later the not-so-subtle differences between Socrates and the rest still passed large numbers of people by; the advocate Aeschines, for example, was still referring to him as 'Socrates the Sophist.'

But major differences there were. First of all, he took no fee for his discussions with the young and others. I say 'discussions', and that brings me to another difference. Socrates, unlike the majority of the Sophists, had no body of knowledge to convey to others, about the art of speaking or about anything else. His interests lay rather in *investigation*, and in particular investigation by the method of what he himself called 'intellectual midwifery.' For him the essence of sound education lay, not in the filling of a bucket (i.e. someone else's mind) with material, but in the coaxing from the minds of others those ideas of which they had all along been unknowingly pregnant. The technique was that of dialogue between Socrates and his interlocutors, with Socrates always pleading ignorance of the precise answer to the topic under discussion but always happy to participate in any dialogue that might throw light on the matter or even perhaps resolve the problem in question. As Plato portrays him in his dialogues, Socrates operates as a sort of 'first among equals', both subtly guiding the discussion along what he senses will turn out to be fruitful channels and also responding as appropriately as he knows how to the specific concerns and objections of his interlocutors as they emerge and present themselves. He himself is first and foremost a moralist. His interest is in goodness, personal and civic, and a great deal of his time is spent trying to get his interlocutors to define individual virtues, or if you like individual aspects of such goodness. So for example in Plato's dialogue *Laches* Socrates discusses with two famous Athenian generals the nature of courage. After a lengthy discussion, the dialogue concludes in a typical way with both of the generals admitting their ignorance of the precise nature of courage, even though both of them have a fair claim to being called conspicuous examples of it. Does that mean that the exercise has ended in failure? Not at all. It has been a great success, because both men have been brought face to face with their own ignorance—which for Socrates is the beginning of wisdom.

Whether Socrates thought any of the virtues really *were* definable we don't know; all we know is that in those Platonic dialogues where the spirit of Socrates seems most evident he never does come to any positive conclusions in the matter. But that is not to say that he has no strong beliefs of his own, in spite of his frequent and ironic self-deprecation and avowals of ignorance. Perhaps the most famous of these beliefs, if he has not been misrepresented, is the belief that 'virtue is knowledge.' To twentieth-century ears the claim is a strange one, and its corollary even stranger—that is, that no one ever does evil of his own free will; he always does it out of ignorance. The view is a little less paradoxical, I think, if one remembers that in the Greek language the word for 'virtue' and the word for 'efficiency' are one and the same. So a good saxophone-player has what Socrates calls *arete* ('efficiency'), and that efficiency consists of 'know-how' in the matter of saxophone playing. By the same token, says Socrates, a good *person* has *arete* (same word—but this time translate it 'virtue'), and that *arete* too will likewise consist of 'know-how,' this time in the matter of morality. However, even when we are informed of this linguistic reason *why* Socrates may have been led to adhere to such a doctrine, it still remains difficult for many to believe that morality is something one is 'good at' in the way one is 'good at' saxophone playing, and history is full of examples of individuals who knew apparently exactly what the right and just thing to do was yet went ahead and did precisely the opposite. Evidently several of Socrates' contemporaries were as puzzled by Socrates' views in this matter as later generations have been—with consequences I shall be mentioning very shortly.

Among other views which apparently distinguished him from most if not all of the Sophists I should also mention the following: that it is better to suffer evil than to do it; that the worst evil one can inflict on another person is to make him or her a worse person; that the care of one's soul is one's primary obligation; and that *self*-knowledge is the most crucial form of knowledge (as he himself put it in a famous phrase: "the unexamined life is not worth living").

Depending on one's own moral stance, the views I have just outlined will be looked upon as at worst innocuous and at best sublime, but either way hardly such—it seems—as to bring down the wrath of Athenians upon Socrates' head. Yet that is just what happened in 399—five years after the end of the Peloponnesian War, when Socrates was tried, found guilty, and executed. Let's look at the matter a little more closely.

You will remember how in the early years of the war, when things were pretty well at a stalemate, the Athenians could afford to attend the theatre and just guffaw at caricatures of Socrates and his like. But as the war progressed the mood changed. To those unprepared to notice subtle but all-important differences (and it could well have been the majority, to judge by Aristophanes' play *The Clouds*) Socrates was a danger to the state, particularly in war-time, when boat-rockers are more than usually suspect. One can *hear* the mutterings. First of all, he taught the young to question everything—even the

115

most sacred beliefs. And then, if not an out-and-out atheist himself, he wasn't prepared, like other decent, god-fearing people, to accept local religious beliefs as absolute truth. He also had this strange, new-fangled view that being a good politician was exactly like being a good flute-player: there was an 'expertise' appropriate to each. The lot-system as a consequence, so dear to Athenian hearts, was nonsense, he claimed, as a technique of civic administration. At a personal level, too, his influence on the young had clearly been pernicious. Look at his pupil Alcibiades, whose personal depravity was a by-word and who had turned traitor to his own country. Or look at that well-known atheist, another of his protégés, Critias. At the end of the war *he* had headed a group of thirty oligarchs who with Sparta's connivance tyrannized the Athenian state for a year and waded in blood, executing hundreds of demo-crats without trial. As it happens, Critias and his henchmen were overthrown, and democracy restored, but it comes as little surprise to find the Athenians, overwhelmed at the loss of their twenty-seven year war with Sparta, and incensed at the bloodbath perpetrated by Quislings like Critias and his gang, looking for–and finding–a scapegoat on whom to vent their rage.

The charge against Socrates was as follows:

Socrates is guilty of not recognizing the gods recognized by the state, and of introducing other, new, divinities. He is also guilty of corrupting the young. The death-penalty is demanded.

If the phrase about 'corrupting the youth' seems vague, it was spelled out in detail a few years later by one Polycrates, one of Socrates' many enemies:

Critias and Alcibiades were two of his closest associates– men who did the greatest of damage to the state. For, as among all the thirty oligarchs the greediest, most violent and most bloodthirsty was Critias, so among all the democrats the most uncontrolled, outrageous and violent was Alcibiades.

Polycrates also points out the noxious connection between Socrates' views on 'efficiency' (moral and otherwise) and his attacks on features of Athens' very democracy, such as the system of selection of civic officials by lot:

> Socrates led his associates to despise the established laws, arguing that it was folly to appoint the rulers of the state by lot, when no-one would be willing to employ a navigator or builder or flute-player who had been selected by lot to do work which, if botched, does far less damage than do political mistakes. Such arguments drive the young to condemn the established political order and make them violent.

And so on. In such an atmosphere Socrates was of course doomed to inevitable conviction, though not, as it happens, to death. At the end of his trial he was free to propose an alternate penalty, and may very well have got away with it had he proposed exile. But for Socrates the Athenian, who had fought three times for his city on the field of battle, and had, as I mentioned earlier, participated actively and courageously in her political life, exile was out of the question, and the ludicrous fine he proposed as an alternate penalty guaranteed his condemnation to death by an even greater majority than had condemned him to death in the first place.

A matchless account of his death by drinking hemlock has been penned for us by Plato:

> By now it was close to sunset. . . . The prison official came in, stepped up to him and said: 'Socrates, I shan't reproach you as I reproach others for being angry with me and cursing, whenever by order of the rulers I direct them to drink the poison. In your time here I've known you for the most generous and gentlest and best of men who have ever come to this place; and now especially, I feel sure it isn't with me that you're

angry, but with others, because you know who are responsible. Well now, you know the message I've come to bring: good-bye, then, and try to bear the inevitable as easily as you can.' And with this he turned away in tears, and went off.

Socrates looked up at him and said: 'Good-bye to you too, and we'll do as you say.' And to us he added: 'What a civil man he is! Throughout my time here he's been to see me, and sometimes talked with me, and been the best of fellows; and now how generous of him to weep for me! But come on, Crito, let's obey him: let someone bring in the poison, if it has been prepared; if not, let the man prepare it.'

Crito said: 'But Socrates, I think the sun is still on the mountains and hasn't yet gone down. And besides, I know of others who've taken the draught long after the order had been given them, and after dining well and drinking plenty, and even in some cases enjoying themselves with those they fancied. Be in no hurry, then: there's still time left.'

Socrates said: 'It's reasonable for those you speak of to do those things—because they think they gain by doing them; for myself, it's reasonable *not* to do them; because I think I'll gain nothing by taking the draught a little later: I'll only earn my own ridicule by clinging to life, and being sparing when there's nothing more left. Go on now; do as I ask, and nothing else.'

Hearing this, Crito nodded to the boy who was standing nearby. The boy went out, and after spending a long time away he returned, bringing the man who was going to administer the poison, and was carrying it ready-pounded in a cup. When he saw the man, Socrates said: 'Well, my friend, you're an expert in these things: what must one do?'

'Simply drink it,' he said, 'and walk about till heaviness comes over your legs; then lie down, and it will act of itself.' And with this he held out the cup to Socrates.

He took it perfectly calmly, Echecrates, without a tremor, or any change of colour or countenance; but looking up at the man, and fixing him with his customary stare, he said: 'What do you say to pouring someone a libation from this drink? Is it allowed or not?'

'We only prepare as much as we judge the proper dose, Socrates,' he said.

'I understand,' he said, 'but at least one may pray to the gods, and so one should, that the removal from this world to the next will be a happy one; that is my own prayer: so may it be.' With these words he pressed the cup to his lips, and drank it off with good humour and without the least distaste.

Till then most of us had been fairly well able to restrain our tears; but when we saw he was drinking, that he'd actually drunk it, we could do so no longer. In my own case, the tears came pouring out in spite of myself, so that I covered my face and wept for myself–not for him, no, but for my own misfortune in being deprived of such a man for a companion. Even before me, Crito had moved away, when he was unable to restrain his tears. And Apollodorus, who even earlier had been continously in tears, now burst forth into such a storm of weeping and grieving, that he made everyone present break down except Socrates himself.

But Socrates said: 'What a way to behave, my friends! Why, it was mainly for this reason that I sent the women away, so that they shouldn't make this sort of trouble; in fact, I've heard one should die in silence. Come now, calm yourselves and have strength.'

When we heard this, we were ashamed and checked our tears. He walked about, and when he said that his legs felt heavy he lay down on his back–as the man told him–and then the man, this one who'd given him the poison, felt him, and after an interval examined his feet and legs; he then pinched his foot hard and asked if he could feel it, and Socrates said no. After that he felt his shins once more; and moving upwards in this way, he showed us that he was becoming cold and numb. He went on feeling him, and said that when the coldness reached his heart, he would be gone.

By this time the coldness was somewhere in the region of his abdomen, when he uncovered his face—it had been covered over—and spoke; and this was in fact his last utterance: 'Crito,' he said, 'we owe a cock to Asclepius: please pay the debt, and don't neglect it.'

'It shall be done,' said Crito; 'have you anything else to say?' To this question he made no answer, but after a short interval he stirred, and when the man uncovered him his eyes were fixed; when he saw this, Crito closed his mouth and his eyes.

And that, Echecrates, was the end of our companion, a man who, among those of his time we know, was—so we should say—the best, the wisest too, and the most just.

Socrates' most famous pupil was Plato. Born around 428 B.C., when the Peloponnesian War had been going on for three years, he was twenty-four or so when he saw his city finally defeated, and twenty-nine when he saw the same city first try and then execute his teacher Socrates. He was of aristocratic birth, and might under normal circumstances have been expected to play a prominent part in Athens' political life. He might also have been expected, given his background, to favour (in the best of all possible worlds) some sort of oligarchy, rather than democracy, like his ultimately infamous uncle Critias. But whatever his intentions and views, in 399, with the death of Socrates, he gave up in despair, having seen the excesses *both* of democrats *and* of oligarchs, and saying in effect 'A plague on both your houses.' He retired completely from public life, to devote himself to perpetuating the memory of Socrates by writing of him, and dreaming all the while of a better political constitution, without the drawbacks that he saw in constitutions like those of Sparta and Athens—but particularly Athens. For the first few years he wrote dialogues, which recreate in priceless detail what was undoubtedly both the spirit and substance of discussions held many years before by Socrates and his friends and pupils. By the time he was forty or so, however, he was beginning to move out from under the shadow of Socrates, and strong views of his own were starting to emerge. The negative endings of the earlier dialogues—in which what is ultimately achieved is an admission all round of how ignorant we are of the topic in question—are now replaced with more confident and positive ones. What Socrates might have believed on instinct, Plato at forty apparently believed was undeniably the case, and it's this: that Socrates' inquiries into the nature of goodness in its various manifestations by means of the technique of definition referred to something *real*. These real things Plato called Forms. So, for example, a just man, a just act and a just society were all such because they 'shared in', or 'imitated' (as he put it) the *form* 'Justice', which was not itself an entity in space and time, but a timeless, unchanging entity, whose function it was to ground the real in all its modes.

With such a Form as his guiding light, Plato proceeded to write what is perhaps his most famous dialogue, *The Republic*, in which (*via* the *persona* of Socrates) he describes with confidence and fervour what a truly just society would look like, were it ever to exist, and what a truly just human being would be like as well. It's an extraordinary document, that has attracted about equal amounts of praise and reprobation. Critics excoriate it as at best a piece of self-deception and at worst a fraud: wittingly or unwittingly, they say, Plato has used the 'cover' of a particularly implausible philosophical theory to construct a supposedly 'just' society that is merely a society in keeping with his own aristocratic prejudices. Friends by contrast see it as a literary and moral masterpiece, in which Plato carries to its sublime conclusion Socrates' contention that the only defensible form of society is one which makes its citizens better human beings. Whichever interpretation is more correct (and I think a good case can be put up for either side), Plato's just society is undoubtedly an 'ordered society', not an egalitarian one. Those who rule in it, however, do so, he says, because they have the talent, education and *virtuousness* to do so, and have as their unswerving objective the good of the entire society, not their own aggrandizement. It's an 'aristocracy' in what for Plato is the only defensible sense of the word: a society ruled by 'the best people' in the sense of 'those people who have been shown by rigorous testing to be intellectually and morally the best-equipped to rule.' (Socrates, we can be sure, would have applauded.) This point about the intellectual ability and unimpeachable moral probity of the rulers must, I think, be stressed, not least because in our own century a régime like that of Hitler tried to use the *Republic* as some sort of prototype for its own particular type of Brave New World. Surface affinities between Plato's and Hitler's societies there undoubtedly are, and it makes large tracts of the *Republic* depressing reading; but a fair-minded critic will in my estimation resist the temptation simply to equate the two. Whatever one thinks of the detailed account of Plato's concept of a Just Society, the purity and nobility of his *goal* – a society of maximum individual and civic *virtuousness*, which for him is identical to maximum individual and civic *contentment* – is in my estimation unsurpassed, and absolves his Ideal State forever from all but the most trivial comparison with squalid and mean-minded autocracies. If Plato is, in terms of *practical* politics, talking nonsense – and he may be – it is at least the nonsense of probity, not of malice.

As it happens, a sobering set of events seems to have convinced Plato that his portrait of a Just Society was likely to remain forever that – an unrealizable ideal. On two (and perhaps three) occasions he was invited to the court of the Tyrant of Syracuse, ostensibly in order to implement his ideas on a Just Society, but the squabbling and infighting that soon broke out among the courtiers made him realize how far his ideals remained from the realities of human nature, and he returned to the safer and less dramatic business of writing. About the same time he also seems to have lost a certain amount of confidence in his famous Theory of Forms, perhaps because of the constant criticism of it by one of his brightest pupils, the young Aristotle. Certainly the dialogues he writes from this time on are with rare exceptions more tentative and hesitant than before, and his last great work, *The Laws*, is the product of a sober and somewhat disillusioned old man who admits that this second and final attempt at an outline of a Just Society is essentially the outline of a *second-best* society; the ideal of his earlier years he now openly states is unattainable.

But I hesitate to leave him on a note which is only a faint and rather dispiriting echo of his earlier passion and idealism. A happier memory, and one more characteristic of the man in his more optimistic prime of life, is a passage from the *Symposium*, in which the priestess Diotima tells the young Socrates how to use things beautiful as the stepping-stone to the vision of the Form Beauty, or Beauty-in-itself.

> The candidate for initiation into the higher mysteries of love cannot, if his efforts are to be rewarded, begin too early to devote himself to the beauties of the body. First of all, if his preceptor instructs him as he should, he will fall in love with the beauty of one individual body, so that his passion may give life to noble discourse. Next he must consider how nearly related the beauty of any one body is to the beauty of any other, when he will see that if he is to devote himself to loveliness of form it will be absurd to deny that the beauty of each and every body is the same.
>
> Next he must grasp that the beauties of the body are as nothing to the beauties of the soul, so that wherever he meets

with spiritual loveliness, even in the husk of an unlovely body, he will find it beautiful enough to fall in love with and to cherish—and beautiful enough to quicken in his heart a longing for such discourse as tends toward the building of a noble nature. And from this he will be led to contemplate the beauty of laws and institutions. And when he discovers how nearly every kind of beauty is akin to every other he will conclude that the beauty of the body is not, after all, of such great moment.

And next, his attention should be diverted from institutions to the sciences, so that he may know the beauty of every kind of knowledge. And thus, by scanning beauty's wide horizon, he will be saved from a slavish and illiberal devotion to the individual loveliness of a single boy, a single man, or a single institution. And, turning his eyes toward the open sea of beauty, he will find in such contemplation the seed of the most fruitful discourse and the loftiest thought, and reap a golden harvest of philosophy, until, confirmed and strengthened, he will come upon one single form of knowledge, the knowledge of the beauty I am about to speak of.

Whoever has been initiated so far in the mysteries of Love and has viewed all these aspects of the beautiful in due succession, is at last drawing near the final revelation. And now, Socrates, there bursts upon him that wondrous vision which is the very soul of the beauty he has toiled so long for. It is an everlasting loveliness which neither comes nor goes, which neither flowers nor fades, for such beauty is the same on every hand, the same then as now, here as there, this way as that way, the same to every worshipper as it is to every other.

Nor will his vision of the beautiful take the form of a face, or of hands, or of anything that is of the flesh. It will be neither words, nor knowledge, nor a something that exists in something else, such as a living creature or the earth, or the heavens, or anything that is—but subsisting of itself in an eternal oneness, while every lovely thing partakes of it in such sort that, however much the parts may wax and wane, it will be neither more nor less, but still the same inviolable whole.

And so, when his precribed devotion to boyish beauties has carried our candidate so far that the universal beauty dawns upon his inward sight, he is almost within reach of the final revelation. And this is the way, the only way, he must approach, or be led toward, the sanctuary of Love. Starting from individual beauties, the quest for the universal beauty must find him ever mounting the heavenly ladder, stepping from rung to rung—that is, from bodily beauty to the beauty of institutions, from institutions to learning, and from learning in general to the special lore that pertains to nothing but the beautiful itself—until at last he comes to know what beauty is.

And if, my dear Socrates, man's life is ever worth the living, it is when he has attained this vision of the very soul of beauty. And once you have seen it, you will never be seduced again by the charm of gold, of dress, you will care nothing for the beauties that used to take your breath away and kindle such a longing in you, and many others like you, Socrates, to be always at the side of the beloved, so that you would be content, if it were possible, to deny yourself the grosser necessities of meat and drink, so long as you were with him.

But if it were given to man to gaze on beauty's very self—unsullied, unalloyed, and freed from the mortal taint that haunts the frailer loveliness of flesh and blood—if, I say, it were given to man to see the heavenly beauty face to face, would you call his an unenviable life, whose eyes had been opened to the vision, and who had gazed upon it in true contemplation until it had become his own forever?

And remember, it is only when he discerns beauty itself through what makes it visible that a man will be quickened with true, and not apparent virtue—for it is virtue's self that quickens him, not virtue's semblance. And when he has brought forth and reared this perfect virtue, he shall be called the friend of god, and if ever it is given to man to put on immortality, it shall be given to him.

In the so-called "Raphael Rooms" of the Vatican Museum there is a painting by Raphael called 'The School of Athens.' In it we see Plato pointing up to heaven—and the *Symposium* passage just quoted gives us some idea why. At Plato's side is his most famous pupil Aristotle—and *he* is pointing firmly down towards the ground! It seems to me a poignant and accurate description of the difference between the other-worldly mind of the one and the more realistic mind of the other.

At the age of eighteen the young Aristotle had come from Northern Greece to Athens as a pupil in Plato's Academy. From the beginning he was brilliant and formidable, and something of a thorn in Plato's side. He was particularly critical, from the outset, of the Theory of Forms, and his criticisms were so successful that as far as I know the Theory has never been held by any significant philosopher since. But that was only the beginning. As the years passed he put together as complete a system of philosophy as the world has ever seen, and even his greatest critics never fail to be impressed. Convinced that no form of reasoning about the world and our place in it can be of much value unless it can be shown to be sound, he wrote the first books of logic, in which he laid down what he took to be the demonstrably accurate and valid rules of sound reasoning, applicable at all times, in all places, and under all circumstances. Faced with the question, "What is real? and what can be known about it?" he replied, contradicting his great teacher, that the *world* is real (not the Forms) and that *it*, rather than the Forms, is the object of knowledge. It was a major shift of emphasis. For Plato the world had been at best partly real, and an object of at best changing opinion;

hence his own gravitation away from this world to that other putative world, the world of Forms. Aristotle, by contrast, is firmly anchored in *this* universe and beams his searching intelligence on every feature of it. He looks at its cause and sustainer, the Self-Activating Intellect which moves the outermost sphere of the universe; he looks at its physical structures, from the stars and planets to the basic units of matter; he looks in enormous detail at its living creatures; he looks finally at man in the universe, and at man specifically as a member of society, and talks at length of the rules for human conduct that form part and parcel of his philosophical system. Those rules turn out to coincide remarkably closely with a vision that we have seen emerging throughout the period I have been discussing. The historian Thucydides, it will be recalled, talked at length of the importance of moderation, and of Athens' tendency to neglect it; the great dramatists Aeschylus, Sophocles and Euripides wrote with fervour on the same theme; and it is of course central to the philosophers Socrates and Plato. All are agreed that the happiest and fullest life for man is the life of goodness in the widest possible sense: a life of personal virtue lived in an environment in which he contributes the maximum to the common good and benefits the maximum in return. The 'virtue' in question, says Aristotle, following in the tradition of his predecessors, will almost always consist of a moderate stance, or as he put it, a 'mean between extremes'. If there is a characteristically Greek contribution to the science of human conduct, this is surely that contribution.

A great deal more could be said about Athens' philosophers, but the time has come to draw the strands of these talks together and formulate some tentative conclusions. I selected three aspects of the Greek achievement for discussion: her political theory and practice, as instanced especially in Athenian democracy; her dramatic art; and the writings of the three most famous of her philosophers. A few concluding words on each of these items are called for.

Talking first of Athenian democracy, we might begin with a hypothetical question: "If conditions were ripe for it, is Athenian democracy the sort of political constitution that we would wish to return to?" The straight answer would have to be a categorical 'No!', on the simple grounds that such democracy was achieved at much too high a price—and by that I mean the chattel-status of a great segment of the population (the slaves, male and female) and the exclusion from political life of the entire *female* half of the adult population that was free. Even if we overlook this problem (and who reasonably could?), there is much in the Athenian system that we have learned from and clearly bettered. In the matter of law, for example, our juries consist of a manageable dozen citizens, not hundreds. The conduct of trials is more carefully controlled, with techniques to guard against irrelevant evidence, and laws of libel to protect against noxious evidence; and conviction is of course on a unanimous vote, not merely on a simple majority vote. In the matter of civic office the world has agreed with Socrates that the lot-system is an absurdity, and no subsequent democracy has to my knowledge ever adopted it. The same might be said for the non-renewable nature of the tenure of such civic posts; most have considered it an inefficient use of the available talent and a barrier to the accumulation of an ongoing body of political experience. And no doubt much more in the way of particular citicisms could be brought forward. Thucydides' great work on the Peloponnesian War, for example, will always stand as a warning to those who feel that the openness of one's political institutions or the existence of wide-ranging individual freedom is any sort of safeguard against the corruption that tends to come with the accumulation of power, or any sort of guarantee of victory against a brave and tenacious enemy, however obnoxious his political system. But when all that is said, Athens still remains as the greater pioneer of the democratic system, for all her inadequacies, and that distinctive title can never be taken from her. If we think we have improved the model somewhat, it is precisely because there was a model to improve, and this has to be a matter for gratitude. And of course in recent years the model has received what may be the highest accolade of all, with the re-introduction into our social and political thinking of the notion of participatory democracy. For centuries it had been assumed that the Athenian system of direct citizenship-participation was something confined to the small boundaries of a city-state, with a relatively small population, and that it was to that degree something unrepeatable. But in recent years we have seen strong moves to reintroduce it at the municipal, if not the federal level of government, and in particular in the smaller and more manageable world of borough-politics. How it will fare is unclear; but its resuscitation at *all* is a tribute to the vigour of the original *Athenian* ideal.

In the matter of drama, the art-form that Athens pioneered has gone on to flourish. The structure and thought-forms have largely vanished, of course, as the specific world of the Greeks has receded from consciousness, but the up-and-down Western tradition of profundity, profanity and dazzling verbal art goes straight back to fifth-century Athens. (One need only mention Shakespeare, a kindred spirit, in artistic brilliance, high seriousness, style, and freedom, to his Athenian predecessors in both tragic and comic drama.) The freedom that Athens provided her playwrights (however uncomfortable the consequences), and the mind-expanding role such playwrights performed in the community, will always serve as a beacon for those for whom art is seen as part of life itself.

What, finally, of the philosophers? Fashions in this matter

come and go, and at different times Greek philosophy in general and individual Greek philosophers in particular have been in and out of fashion. Indeed, it's true to say that there's hardly an argument in Greek philosophy that some other philosopher has not at one time or another subjected to criticism. Why then are the Greek philosophers still read? For the very same reason that thinking people constantly re-view the workings of Athenian democracy. In philosophy as in politics the Greek philosophers swam in new and dangerous currents, and on occasion were violently overwhelmed by them, but the tradition of courageous exploration is their permanent legacy. Under their tutelage Western man moved irreversibly away from a mythological view of the real to a more rational one, and few would deny that this puts us permanently in their debt. Of their individual doctrines much more could be said; but I shall content myself, by way of conclusion, with a single reference once more to that personal and civic goodness that was championed notably and specifically by Socrates, Plato and Aristotle as—ideally—man's greatest happiness, highest achievement, and finest contribution to the world. The spirit of such commitment to goodness, so profound a part of the legacy of so many of Greece's thinkers, is caught as clearly and as movingly as anywhere I know in a short interchange between Socrates and the young Phaedrus at the end of Plato's dialogue of that name. The afternoon has drawn to a close, and with it their discussion. They are sitting by the banks of the river Ilissus, shaded by a plane tree, and Socrates, as must have been his custom on such occasions, concludes the proceedings with an address to the gods of the region:

> SOCRATES: Dear Pan, and all you other gods that dwell in this place, grant that I may become fair within, and that such outward things as I have may not war against the spirit within me. May I count him rich who is wise, and as for gold, may I possess so much of it as only a man of moderation might bear and carry with him.

Is there anything more we can ask for, Phaedrus? The prayer contents me.

PHAEDRUS: Make it a prayer for me too, since friends have all things in common.

SOCRATES: Let us be going.

Selected Bibliography

NOTE: This bibliography covers merely the topics discussed in the book. It is in no way meant to cover all aspects of the history and culture of Ancient Greece. It is also meant as *introductory* reading for interested non-specialists; the books listed do not necessarily include the latest research-opinion on any given topic but do seem to me lively, readable, and reasonably accurate introductions *to* that topic.

General

(a) *Basic Histories of Ancient Greece*

1. J.B. BURY and Russell MEIGGS, *A History of Greece to the Death of Alexander the Great*[4] (London, 1975)
2. N.G.L. HAMMOND, *A History of Greece to 322 B.C.* (Oxford, 1959)
3. Peter GREEN, *Ancient Greece: An Illustrated History* (New York, 1973)

(b) *Introductions to the civilization of Ancient Greece*

1. H.D.F. KITTO, *The Greeks* (Penguin Books, 1951)
2. A.A. ANDREWES, *The Greeks* (London, 1967)

Particular

1 *Beginnings*

1. Robert FITZGERALD (Tr.), *The Odyssey* (Garden City, New York, 1961)
2. Robert FITZGERALD (Tr.), *The Iliad* (Garden City, New York, 1974)
3. Richmond A. LATTIMORE (Tr.), *Greek Lyrics*[2] (Chicago U.P., 1960)
4. Appropriate chapters in Bury, Hammond, Green.

2 *Two Societies*

1. W.G.G. FORREST, *The Emergence of Greek Democracy, 800-400 B.C.* (New York, 1966).

2. W.G.G. FORREST, *A History of Sparta, 950-192 B.C.* (London, 1968)

3. A.H.M. JONES, *Athenian Democracy* (Oxford, 1969)

4. Naphtali LEWIS, *The Fifth Century B.C.* (Toronto, 1971)

5. Appropriate chapters in Bury, Hammond, Green.

3 *War, and the Lessons of War*

1. Rex WARNER (Tr.), *Thucydides: The Peloponnesian War* (Penguin Books, 1972)

2. Appropriate chapters in Bury, Hammond, Green.

4 *The Artistic Achievement*

1. Gilbert MURRAY, *Aeschylus, The Creator of Tragedy* (Oxford, 1940)

2. C.M. BOWRA, *Sophoclean Tragedy* (Oxford, 1944)

3. Gilbert MURRAY, *Euripides and his Age* (introd. by H.D.F. Kitto) (Oxford, 1965; first published 1918)

4. G.M.A. GRUBE, *The Drama of Euripides* (New York, 1961; first published 1941)

5. Gilbert MURRAY, *Aristophanes: A Study* (Oxford, 1933)

6. K.J. DOVER, *Aristophanic Comedy* (Berkeley, 1972)

7. P. DICKINSON (Tr.), *Aristophanes, Plays* (Oxford, 1970)

8. H.D.F. KITTO, *Greek Tragedy: A Literary Study* (London, 1954)

9. D. GRENE and R. LATTIMORE (eds.), *The Complete Greek Tragedies*. 4 Vols. (Chicago, 1974).

10. Philip VELLACOTT (Tr.), *Euripides, The Bacchae and Other Plays* (Penguin Books, 1954).

11. ———, *Euripides, Medea and Other Plays* (Penguin Books, 1963).

12. ———, *Aeschylus, The Oresteian Trilogy* (Penguin Books, 1959).

5 *The Thinkers*

1. J.M. ROBINSON, *An Introduction to Early Greek Philosophy* (Boston, 1968)